HELPING
YOURSELF
WITH
NUMEROLOGY

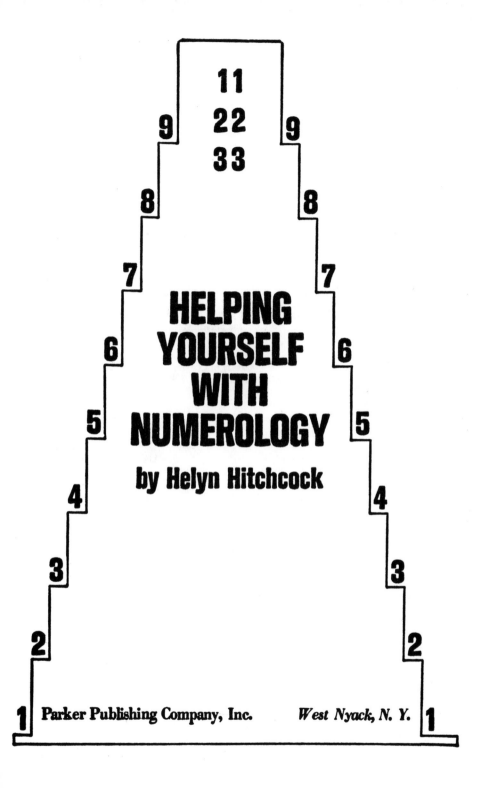

11
22
33

9   9

8   8

7   7

HELPING
YOURSELF
WITH
NUMEROLOGY

by Helyn Hitchcock

6   6

5   5

4   4

3   3

2   2

Parker Publishing Company, Inc.   *West Nyack, N. Y.*

1   1

Library of Congress
Catalog Card Number: 72-172406

20   19   18   17

10   9   8   RWD CLASSICS PBK

This book is a reference work based on research by
the author. The opinions expressed herein are not
necessarily those of or endorsed by the Publisher.

ISBN   0-13-386756-0   RWD

CLASSIC PBK

Printed in the United States of America

What This Book Can Do for You

By using the knowledge of Numerology gained through reading and applying the programs in this book, you can discover for yourself what talents you already possess, and what obstacles hinder your progress to succeed at your desired goals.

You will be able to figure out when is the best time for you to forge ahead with a project, and when it is feasible for you to wait until more favorable numbers are indicated. You can ascertain from your numbers whether a certain person is the right one for you to marry. By studying the secret desire numbers of your mate or friend, you can learn to understand that person better.

You will learn how to be your own numerologist, and how to cast your own numeroscope to get the answers for steering a successful course in your daily life.

WHAT IS NUMEROLOGY?

Numerology, or the Science of Numbers, had its origin in symbols used to express the ideas of primitive man. It not only is based on numbers with a quantitative value, such as two plus two equals four, but it exists even today because the numbers or symbols have a metaphysical value with a definite meaning within them denoting inner dynamic characteristics shaping one's destiny. Long before alphabets were invented to correspond to their respective numbers, ancient scholars studied the science of numbers for guidance in daily living.

NUMEROLOGY IS AN EASY ART

This book is both easy to follow and a practical guide for your daily use. It will show you step by step how, in a few minutes, you can set up a chart and figure your own numeroscope. It will point out for example:

1. What days are best for you to apply for a new job, or start a new venture.
2. When to buy property or invest in a business.
3. What experiences you cannot avoid meeting, and what obstacles you must overcome.
4. How to choose your marriage partner.
5. The best date to get married.
6. The best place for you to make your home.
7. What cities and companies want what you have to offer.
8. What days are best for you to take a trip.
9. In which line of endeavor or business you will be most successful.
10. You can be the center of attention at a party by quickly jotting down the names and dates of birth of guests, and giving them a quick reading of their characteristics and talents.
11. How a change in your name can help you secure desired success.

YOU CAN KNOW WHAT THE FUTURE
HOLDS FOR YOU THROUGH NUMEROLOGY

The unique chapter on how to make predictions in this book is an exclusive feature. It sets out a secret method of foretelling future events through Numerology. To my knowledge, no numerologist has ever given his system for predictions to the general public, for it constitutes his stock in trade in his professional practice. Now you can be enabled to predict future events affecting you, and you can set your successful course of action accordingly.

Helyn Hitchcock

Contents

HELPING
YOURSELF
WITH
NUMEROLOGY

How to Set Up a
Working Chart on Numerology

All charts have keys which unlock their interpretation. Numbers and letters are no exception to this rule, for they are interchangeable. Numbers have been in existence since the beginning of time When alphabets came into being, letters were given their specific value numerically because of the meaning behind them.

WHAT YOU WILL LEARN

In this chapter you will learn how to set up a chart of the nine single digits from one to nine inclusive. You will learn how to put the appropriate letter of the alphabet under each number.

In the following chart or table, each letter vibrates to one of the nine digits. Any compound number is not a digit, even though it can be reduced to a single digit or number.

CHART OR KEY OF NUMBERS AND THEIR
CORRESPONDING LETTERS

The one			The many			The all			Master Numbers
1	2	3	4	5	6	7	8	9	11
A	B	C	D	E	F	G	H	I	22
J	K	L	M	N	O	P	Q	R	33
S	T	U	V	W	X	Y	Z	&	

17

In the above chart A = 1; B = 2; C = 3; D = 4; E = 5; F = 6; G = 7; H = 8; I = 9. Having utilized all of the nine digits we now start learning the second line in which J = 1; K = 2; L = 3; M = 4; N = 5; O = 6; P = 7; Q = 8; R = 9. Since there are only nine basic digits we again start with one, thus, S = 1; T = 2; U = 3; V = 4; W = 5; X = 6; Y = 7; Z = 8. The "&" is not a letter or number, but since many companies have incorporated this symbol into their name, we must have a way of figuring this symbol, which means "AND."

The division of the numbers and letters by a vertical line running between three and four, and between six and seven, suggests the following:

> 1, 2, and 3 are personal numbers termed the "ONE."
>> Their watch word is ME OR MINE. They are interested in the self or the individual.
> 4, 5, and 6 are limited vibrations or the "MANY." Their watchword is YOU. They serve their own family and community.
> 7, 8, and 9 are the universal vibrations termed the "ALL." They serve humanity without distinction.

Eleven, twenty-two and thirty-three are added to the chart, but they are not vibrations corresponding to any particular letter. They should be treated as super vibrations of their single digits of 11 (1 + 1 = 2), 22 (2 + 2 = 4); and 33 (3 + 3 = 6).

HOW TO READ A NAME IN NUMEROLOGY

To learn to read a name or the total of all names, there is a definite rule to follow, namely: All numbers must be reduced to a final single digit unless the total is one of the master numbers— eleven or twenty-two. If so, they are retained and not reduced. You reduce numbers by adding the numbers until you reach a single number result, or digit. For instance, if the total of all of your letter digits were twenty-four, you would add this compound number together to get a single digit, thus (2 + 4 = 6). If the total were eleven or twenty-two, you would keep them as such even though they were combined with another number, such as 22-4 or 11-5. For example, numbers should not be reduced to eight (2 + 2 + 4), or seven (1 + 1 + 5).

HOW TO SET UP A CHART OF YOUR NAME
ON NUMEROLOGY

You must figure each name separately in the following manner:

Step 1. Consult the chart of letters and numbers on page 17 and place the appropriate number under the letters of your first name. Now reduce this to a single total, adding the separate numbers.

Step 2. Follow the same procedure with the second or middle name, reducing this to a single total.

Step 3. Place the correct number under the letters of your last or surname. Reduce this to a single digit.

Step 4. Add together the totals of the first, middle, and last names. Reduce these until you arrive at a single digit or total.

If there are several middle names, you should drop them entirely or combine them and treat them as one. Many middle names lose their significance because the effect is too scattered.

SOME PRACTICE EXAMPLES FOR CHARTING NAMES

Get out your pencil and scratch pad for working out some examples charting names. We'll set up an imaginary name, as an example, to show you how to set up and figure your own name. Let's pretend that your first name is Margaret. Put the name Margaret on your scratch pad and then consult the table or chart (page 17) for the specific numerical value of each letter. Place these numbers directly under the letters.

Thus:

$$\begin{array}{cccccccc} M & A & R & G & A & R & E & T \\ 4 & 1 & 9 & 7 & 1 & 9 & 5 & 2 \end{array}$$

$$(3+8) = \frac{38}{11}$$

M has the value of 4; A-1; R-9; G-7; A-1; R-9; E-5; T-2.
These numbers total thirty-eight, namely, $(4+1+9+7+1+9+5+2=38)$. You must now reduce this

compound number to a single digit by adding the digits together, thus $(3 + 8 = 11)$, which still is a compound number. Ordinarily you would again reduce the eleven to a single digit, but since it is a master number (11), you should leave it as eleven and not reduce it to two, namely $(1 + 1 = 2)$.

Now you should set up your middle name in the same way as Margaret. Let's imagine that it is Alice. Place the numerical value or number under each letter.

Example:

$$
\begin{array}{ccccc}
A & L & I & C & E \\
1 & 3 & 9 & 3 & 5 \\
\end{array}
$$
$$
(2+1)= \dfrac{21}{3}
$$

Consulting the chart or key on page 17, you will learn that $A = 1$; $L = 3$; $I = 9$; $C = 3$; and $E = 5$; Adding these together you will arrive at the compound number of twenty-one, thus $(1 + 3 + 9 + 3 + 5 = 21)$. This should again be reduced to a single total. You will do this by adding together $(2 + 1 = 3)$. The single digit of three is the numerological total of the name Alice.

Now imagine your last or hereditary name is Johnson. Put this on your scratch pad. Again consult the key or chart on page 17 and set up your surname as you did your first name (Margaret), and your middle name (Alice).

Example:

$$
\begin{array}{ccccccc}
J & O & H & N & S & O & N \\
1 & 6 & 8 & 5 & 1 & 6 & 5 \\
\end{array}
$$
$$
\dfrac{32}{5} \quad (3+2=5)
$$

Again looking at the key, you will find that $J = 1$; $O = 6$; $H = 8$; $N = 5$; $S = 1$; $O = 6$; and $N = 5$. Put these numbers on your pad under the letters of Johnson. Now add these figures together. You will arrive at thirty-two, thus $(1 + 6 + 8 + 5 + 1 + 6 + 5 = 32)$.

Reduce this to a single total, namely (3 + 2 = 5).

All super or master numbers should be reduced to a single digit unless they occur as a total. If an individual is not living up to his master numbers, he will revert to the lesser aspects of his number, such as eleven will reduce to two, twenty-two will reduce to four; and thirty-three to six. The potential of the super number remains constant, but in the background. A master number eleven could be degrading, and a twenty-two might be a criminal. A twenty-two who does not live up to·his high possibilities is often found as a clerk in an office, a bookkeeper, or a manual laborer. There's nothing degrading about being a laborer, but if you were born with much greater potentials, you should try to live up to your numbers.

Now we'll add all of the names together, not forgetting the separate totals of each name.

Example:

$$
\begin{array}{ccc}
\text{M A R G A R E T} & \text{A L I C E} & \text{J O H N S O N} \\
\underline{4\ 1\ 9\ 7\ 1\ 9\ 5\ 2} & \underline{1\ 3\ 9\ 3\ 5} & \underline{1\ 6\ 8\ 5\ 1\ 6\ 5} \\
\underline{38} & \underline{21} & \underline{32} \\
11\quad + & 3\quad + & 5\ =
\end{array}
$$

$$
(11 + 3 + 5) = \underline{(11 + 8)}
$$
$$
10
$$

If you actually had the name of Margaret Alice Johnson, you would add the subtotals of Margaret (11), Alice (3), and Johnson (5) together to arrive at the final total of (11 + 8) = 10.

There is an underlying total of ten made up of eleven and eight. The ten in this case would be stronger than a plain ten or one, because it is made up of a master number eleven and an eight.

SEVERAL EXAMPLES FOR YOU TO WORK OUT

As a first attempt you should concentrate on setting up your own full given name at birth. Be sure to follow the four steps enumerated under, "How to Set Up a Chart of Your Name on Numerology" on a previous page. After you have completed it, recheck it with the table to eliminate any error. Then you may want to set up the names of other members of your household and figure these to get a total.

For extra practice, I'll set up the names of several famous individuals. After you have figured these, compare your calculations with mine to see if you have been accurate.

The Following Names Are Examples:

JACK WILLIAM NICKLAUS

ELIZABETH FRANCES TAYLOR

GUY ALBERT LOMBARDO

Be sure to figure these names yourself before you peek at my calculations for verification.

Put the name Jack on your scratch pad. Consult the chart, and place the correct number under each letter.

Thus·

J A C K

<u>1 1 3 2</u>

=7

J has the value of 1; A = 1; C = 3; K = 2. These numbers total seven, namely (1 + 1 + 3 + 2 = 7). The total single digit of Jack is seven.

Now set up his middle name of William.

Thus:

WI LLI AM

<u>5 9 3 3 9 1 4</u>

<u>34</u>

(3 + 4) = 7

Place the numerical value of each number under the corresponding letter of the name William. Use the same method as you did for Jack. The name of William totals thirty-four. Since this is a compound number you must reduce this to a single digit be adding the two numbers together, thus (3 + 4 = 7). The single digit of William is seven, the same as the total name of Jack.

Now set up his last or hereditary name of Nicklaus.

$$\text{N I C K L A U S}$$

$$\underline{5\ 9\ 3\ 2\ 3\ 1\ 3\ 1}$$

$$\begin{array}{r} 27 \\ (2 + 7) = \quad 9 \end{array}$$

Place the correct numerical value of each letter under the corresponding letter of the name Nicklaus, just as you did for Jack and William. The total of Nicklaus is twenty-seven, which must be reduced to a single digit, namely (2 + 7 = 9). The single digit for Nicklaus is nine.

Now add all of the totals of each separate name together to get a single name total or digit.

Example:

$$\underline{\text{J A C K}} \quad \underline{\text{W I L L I A M}} \quad \underline{\text{N I C K L A U S}}$$

$$7 \quad + \quad 7 \quad + \quad 9 \quad =$$

$$23 = (2 + 3 = 5)$$

Jack (7) plus William (7) plus Nicklaus (9) equals twenty-three, which must be reduced to a single digit, namely (2 + 3 = 5). Five is the total digit for the name of Jack William Nicklaus.

Now check the figures of your second name of Elizabeth Frances Taylor with mine.

Consult the table and place the correct numerical value under each letter of her first name of ELIZABETH.

Example:

$$\text{E L I Z A B E T H}$$

$$\underline{5\ 3\ 9\ 8\ 1\ 2\ 5\ 2\ 8}$$

$$\begin{array}{r} \underline{43} \\ 7 \end{array}$$

The first name of Elizabeth has a total of forty-three, which becomes seven when it is reduced, because $(4 + 3 = 7)$.

Now follow the same procedure for her middle name of Frances.

Thus:

F R A N C E S

6 9 1 5 3 5 1

$$\frac{30}{3}$$

The middle name of Frances has a total of thirty, which reduces to three because $(3 + 0 = 3)$.

Now set up her last name of Taylor, following the same method.

T A Y L O R

2 1 7 3 6 9

$$\frac{28}{\frac{10}{1}}$$

The last name of Taylor has a total of twenty-eight, which reduces first to ten and then again to one. The single digit of Taylor is one. Now add the totals of each separate name together.

ELIZABETH   FRANCIS   TAYLOR

7   +   3   +   1   =   11

We do *not* reduce the eleven to two because eleven is a master number total.

How nearly correct were you step for step in your calculations of Elizabeth Frances Taylor, the famous actress?

Now let's figure the third or last name you were given for a sample. Guy Albert Lombardo's orchestra is still playing for the pleasure of many.

GUY

7 3 7

$$\frac{17}{8}$$

In figuring his first name of Guy, the total numerical value is seventeen, which when reduced becomes eight because one plus seven is eight.

ALBERT

1 3 2 5 9 2

22

His middle name of Albert has a total of twenty-two. As stated previously, when a master number occurs as a total of a name, you should not reduce it. Remember, the master numbers are eleven, twenty-two, and thirty-three. Therefore, the total should be kept as twenty-two and not reduced to four. The total of Albert is twenty-two.

LOMBARDO

3 6 4 2 1 9 4 6

$$\frac{35}{8}$$

The total name of Lombardo adds to thirty-five, which reduces to eight because three plus five is eight. The total of all of his names is: Guy (8) plus Albert (22) plus Lombardo (8) = 22 + 8 + 8 = 22 + 16 = 22 + 7.

Thus:

GUY ALBERT LOMBARDO

8   +   22   +   8   =

(22 + 16) = (22 + 1 + 6) = (22 + 7)

What was your score this time? Working these examples should help you check your own name. I suggest you try to memorize the chart of the nine digits and their letters so that they will be as familiar to you as reciting the multiplication table. This will save your constantly referring to the basic table.

TWO

General Meaning of Numbers

HOW TO KNOW WHAT THE SYMBOLS TELL YOU

You could not expect to receive any benefit from setting up your name if you didn't know what the name or its corresponding numbers mean. You must be able to understand and interpret your name and numbers by finding out what their symbols tell you in order for them to have any significance for you. When you can skillfully analyze your numbers, then you are on the right track toward becoming a meaningful numerologist.

In this chapter you will learn the general meaning of numbers. Later on in this book, you will also be able to apply your knowledge to other specific instances and interpretations.

YOU ARE SIMILAR NUMEROLOGICALLY TO A PERSON WITH YOUR SAME NAME TOTAL IN GENERAL CHARACTERISTICS ONLY

If your total name reduces to a number One, you will be similar to a person with the same number total of One in general characteristics, but not in specific details. The "real you" will stand out when your whole individual chart, with respect to its many aspects, is analyzed and diagnosed and fitted together. If you will read and apply the general meaning of the number total of your full given name, you will find that it will fit you in general aspects.

GENERAL MEANING OF NUMBERS

Numbers are like relatives and friends. Some are harmonious with you, while others will clash.

ZERO: THE MESSENGER OF THE NINE DIGITS

While zero, naught, or the cipher is actually not a number, since it does not designate a quantity, it is the beginning or forerunner of the digits. The symbol *0* signifies the eternal, the universe, and the potential growth from which all of the nine digits evolve. Symbols are still widely used in exact sciences to convey ideas.

Since neither you nor anyone can identify himself as a number zero (0), I have not gone into detail to describe its characteristics in the general meaning of numbers. It is simply a messenger of the nine digits.

Number 1 Characteristics

If you are a number *one*, you are an individualist—independent and determined. Usually you can reach your goal. Being a creator or instigator, you are first in all actions, for you are a leader and a doer. You are Mr. Idea, but you should keep your plans to yourself for you work best alone and quietly. You should cut loose of all family ties, and strike out as a pioneer in a new field.

You have the courage and intelligence to explore the unknown. Having considerable executive ability, you can be the manager or head of a business or enterprise, or the promoter of a movement. You learn by experience more than most numbers, for you dislike being given advice. You are proud, resent criticism, and often display your temper, or you may have emotional upsets. You are inclined to boss others, and you want your own way.

If you are negatively inclined, you should guard against being lazy, cynical, or even a dreamer, for these traits lead to procrastination and insecurity.

You may be self-centered, for most *ones* represent the *Me First* principle. You've often heard the expression: "I'm going to look out for number one," and you can be sure you'll do just that, for you are well able to stand on your own feet.

You can succeed as an inventor, aviator, engineer, teacher, salesman, leader, head of a business, pioneer, or in the automotive or electrical field.

Number 2 Characteristics

If you are a number *two* you are dual in nature. Since you can see both sides of a situation, you serve as a balance between opposing forces and would qualify as an excellent arbitrator or peace maker.

You are timid, sensitive, and often lack self-confidence. Therefore, you prefer to work in the background. As a statistician you can collect information and evaluate it.

You are emotional in nature, and often turn to music. You have a deep sense of rhythm and harmony. As a *two*, you work better with a partner or in a subordinate occupation than in an individual capacity.

You could excel at being a diplomat, for you are tactful, kind, and tolerant.

A *two* is the opposite of the masculine *one*, for a *two* illustrates the feminine principle of receptivity. You are cooperative and patient. You could be found carrying a flag of truce, for you are a harbinger of peace. You prefer to be the follower.

You could succeed as a statistician, accountant, clerk, diplomat, librarian, musician, politician, painter, or peacemaker.

Number 3 Characteristics

If you are a number *three*, you take life as it comes, love pleasure, and are essentially youthful.

You have the talent for expressing yourself well in speaking, writing, or acting. As a number *three* you are gifted in being creative, but you are not noted for being practical. You dream big ventures, for you think on a large scale, but you always want to inject beauty into every situation. Having a quick and keen mind, you learn easily. You can do almost anything you decide you want to accomplish. You are endowed with super-imagination, and for this reason you may gravitate to the entertainment field. This can lead to many opportunities and financial success. Many fields of endeavor are open to a number *three*. Because of this you must be careful not to scatter your talents like an octopus in many directions. You must also guard against being too talkative, and so cause strained situations, and even loss of friends. Very few *threes* are accused of worrying or being depressed, for as a *three* you enjoy social life. Expression is your key note.

There are three types of *threes*. One is the studious or mental variety; another is social; and the third type is emotional and slightly unstable.

You could succeed as a speaker, writer, actor, painter, musician, humorist, entertainer, comedian, beautician, or salesman, especially of health and beauty products.

Number 4 Characteristics

If you are a number *four,* you deserve the label "Salt of the earth," for you are dependable, practical, and reliable. You are not apt to stumble when you walk, for your eyes and feet will be centered squarely on the ground, not in the clouds. As a number *four,* you possess more than your share of good common sense. You may not be a mental wizard, but you are a stable, solid citizen, who is a hard worker, and conservative both in your viewpoints and in dealing with finances. If you disagree with another's policy or actions, you can be as stubborn as a mule, refusing to budge.

As a number *four* you are an excellent disciplinarian. You could manage others, or discipline yourself equally well to carry out your aims, for you are not afraid of hard work or manual labor. You belong before the public. Often you will be employed by the government in some civic capacity, or you may engage in politics. You are orderly, patriotic, systematic, and excellent at handling routine matters. You are not the creative type, for you lack the necessary imagination.

You could succeed as a contractor, farmer, mechanic, draftsman, government employee, clerk, laborer, factory worker or foreman, accountant, or politician.

Number 5 Characteristics

If you are a number *five,* you desire freedom and expansion in all things. You are versatile and changeable. Being the number of experience, you learn by promoting new ideas, for which you have an insatiable curiosity. Your progress will consist of moving forward and onward, having the courage to let go of the old, and being willing to learn the untried.

You often are impulsive, restless, and quick to act. You love adventure, and will even tread in quicksand, for you do things on the spur of the moment without thinking things out. You know how to make a party lively, and you can keep up an interesting conversation.

As a number *five* you are a super salesman. You like to speculate, taking a chance with whatever money you possess. You may engage in some field of athletics and excel at it. You like the company of the opposite sex.

You could run a travel bureau or be a guide on a tour around the world. You often drown yourself in social activities.

You have a serious side to your nature. You are willing to try anything new. This courage can develop into something advantageous for the general good of the public.

You could succeed as a salesman, psychologist, investigator, writer, detective, traveler, insurance adjuster, or a dealer in stocks and bonds.

Number 6 Characteristics

If you are a number *six*, you crave love, friends, and companionship. You are devoted to your family to the extent that you often smother them with love and protection.

Serving in the community gives you great pleasure. You do not like to be alone, but prefer to be in a crowd.

While you strive for peace and harmony, you do enjoy a stiff argument as long as no one remains angry when the debate is resolved. You like to see a home run smoothly and orderly. You also like beautiful things and surroundings. Being cautious in money matters, you will invest only in what appears to be foolproof.

You are liked by most people, for you are kind and tolerant. At times you can become stubborn and argumentative if anyone disagrees with you. You are prone to worry, often needlessly. Since you like comfort, you prefer to fall into a routine rather than submit to being uprooted and moved.

Having a good sense of timing, you often gravitate to a career in music, either singing or playing a musical instrument.

You also delight in decorating your home artistically. While you strive to please others, you require praise, and you need encouragement.

You could succeed as a doctor, nurse, musician, civic worker, homemaker, interior decorator, cook, or teacher.

Number 7 Characteristics

If you are a number *seven*, you are a deep thinker. You will absorb knowledge from practically every source. Being intellectual, scientific, and studious, you never accept a premise unless you have analyzed the situation thoroughly, and reached your own conclusion. You dislike suggestions from others, mainly because you think you are the authority on any subject. You resent injustice, but you should never attempt to get even, for it will act as a boomerang and will hurt you more than the person you try to injure.

You dislike manual labor. You are not as domestic as a number *six*, or as practical as a number *four*. You are spiritually and philosophically inclined. While you may be religious, you often lean toward metaphysics. You want quietude to meditate and live your inner life. You must learn to live alone and not be lonely. You usually will avoid crowds, for you may become upset when subjected to noise and confusion.

You believe that seeking knowledge is second only to acquiring understanding and wisdom. Your keynote is perfection, not popularity. You may appear to be cold and aloof, but this is because you are satisfied with your full inner life. You are an idealist rather than a down to earth individual.

As a number *seven*, you should rely on your intuition and follow your hunches. You can easily detect a deception, or recognize a superficial individual. You love nature, and are fond of animals.

You could succeed as a scientist, teacher, occultist, writer, horticulturist, inventor, lawyer, actor, analyst, or a religious leader.

Number 8 Characteristics

If you are a number *eight*, you should never rely on luck, for you must work hard to earn what you get. Justice should be your keynote. As a number *eight*, you may seem to be restricted. This need not be true if you have learned to discipline yourself. You can have outstanding success by moving cautiously and conservatively, relying on your own judgment, for as a number *eight* you are mental and should be well-balanced. If you live by the golden rule you can earn a place of authority.

The symbol of number *eight* resembles the double circle (8). It is the number of the scales, meaning balance and organization. It is physical or material in aspect, much like the number *four*, but it can reach greater heights. It is more interested in financial success than in spiritual enlightenment, for number *eight* is a business vibration. One foot at a time should be your watchword, for this principle will lead you to expansion and final manifestation.

You could succeed in business in a broad field, such as being the president or manager of a large company. Other lines open for you are as an efficiency expert, industrialist, or a executive. You could also be drawn to business law, banking, acting, or manufacturing. Governmental work, civic affairs, and politics are other branches for you to follow. If you choose a literary career, it usually is that of an editor, publisher, or critic rather than an author, although you could write a "HOW TO" book concerning some phase of business.

Number 9 Characteristics

If you are a number *nine*, you are governed by the symbol of love, representing the highest form of both universal love and love of your neighbor. You crave personal love, but this should not be your aim, for it may prove to be disappointing. You are the big brother of humanity. Being selfless, you will give, even unwisely, when your emotions are aroused, for your motto should be "Do unto others." You are compassionate, broadminded, and idealistic, and can easily sense the difficulties and needs of others to such an extent that you will suffer greatly if another is mistreated or in want.

If your name has many *nines*, you are equipped to cope with all conditions and circumstances on this earth.

Numbers *one* and *nine* are at opposite ends of the numerological totem pole. Number *one* stands for individuality, while number *nine* is symbolical of universality.

You may experience many heartaches, even losing friends, money, and social status if you have not learned to live impersonally.

You could succeed as a doctor, nurse, humanitarian, lawyer, writer, painter, dancer, or in community work serving the public. You feel at home helping others, both financially and in giving service. As an actor you would have deep understanding, and would appeal to the general public.

Master Number 11 Characteristics

If you are a number *eleven*, you are an idealist, a dreamer, and sometimes a mystic. Having much vision, you should be an inspiration to others. You can open doors and help others to greater achievements. Being psychic, you should follow your hunches.

You belong on the platform giving speeches or sermons, for people like to listen to you.

You must learn to be practical and carry out your plans. Otherwise, you are apt to live in the clouds and accomplish nothing.

You must learn to keep appointments, and to be on time for them.

You should think of others first by serving mankind instead of concentrating on affairs which will yield good for only you.

You could succeed as a psychologist, teacher, speaker, writer, philosopher, evangelist, psychoanalyst, missionary, actor, inventor explorer, in radio or TV, an astrologer, or a welfare worker.

Since *eleven* is the higher vibration of *two*, I suggest you read what is written about number *two*. It applies to you as a number *eleven*, but more is expected of you because you have a master number.

Master Number 22 Characteristics

If you are a number *twenty-two* you are a practical idealist. You not only have visions, but you can see things on a large scale and are able to carry out your plans to achieve your goal. As a *twenty-two* you are a master builder, bringing order and system to the world. You are an internationalist. Your power and influence can be far-reaching.

You should launch projects for the benefit of humanity. You could deal in railroads, airplanes, waterways, peace movements, or an international enterprise. You are able to deal with groups effectively.

Much is expected of you, for a *twenty-two* is the highest number possible. If you do not live up to your possibilities, you may revert to living as a *four*.

Since *twenty-two* is the higher vibration of *four*, I suggest that you read what is written about number *four* for it applies to you also. However, your responsibilities are much greater than that of a *four*.

You could succeed as an efficiency expert, ambassador, writer, president, buyer, writer, teacher, diplomat, director of world affairs, or an organizer of public works.

Master Number 33 Characteristics

Thirty-three is too powerful and advanced a number for many individuals to handle at this time. When *thirty-three* is found as a total of a name or birthpath of a person, he is greatly advanced spiritually. He is equal to a Mahatma or Master.

Since few living individuals have attained to this high spiritual status at present, I'll omit the *thirty-three* in my future calculations as a master number.

SUMMARY OF GENERAL MEANING AND CHARACTERISTICS OF NUMBERS IN A NAME

Number

0 = the potential of all numbers. It can be *all* or *no-thing.*

1 = inventor, pioneer, creator, leader, originator, individualist.

2 = peacemaker, diplomat, musician, statistician, clerk, librarian.

3 = artist, speaker, writer, entertainer, humorist.

4 = builder, farmer, government employee, politician, mechanic, clerk.

5 = traveler, salesman, detective, psychologist, adventurer, writer.

6 = teacher, parent, civic worker, doctor, nurse, decorator, cook.

7 = thinker, philosopher, psychic, perfectionist, writer, teacher.

8 = analyst, executive, organizer, business promoter, lawyer, banker, editor.

9 = philanthropist, traveler, healer, humanitarian, minister, actor, doctor.

11 = idealist, speaker, religionist, psychic, writer, diplomat.

22 = internationalist, practical master builder, ambassador, diplomat, president.

33 = avatar, spiritual master, universal leader of a movement.

THREE

How to Analyze Your Name

Your name elements consist of several separate, or distinct names. Therefore, when we allude to your name, we actually mean your first, middle, and last name, but for the sake of brevity in the future, we shall merely refer to your name when we mean names. Each separate name, since it has a vibratory rate, changes the aspects of your total name. This accounts for the fact that individuals, having the same *total* number, often differ greatly in characteristics.

RELATION OF SEPARATE NAMES WITHIN A WHOLE NAME

Your first name, or the one by which you are known, is your *active* name. It is true even if your name consists only of initials, such as: A.P., or even of numbers, like: 483.

Your *middle* name, which is *passive,* is the bridge connecting the active (first) and the family (last) name.

Your *last* or *family name* shows atavistic or hereditary traits. If your middle name, or your nickname, is most frequently used, then that becomes your active, and the first name becomes the passive name. As stated previously, if you have three or four subordinate or middle names, then the influence will be slight because of the scattering of forces. These many names are either omitted entirely or grouped and treated as a whole. The exception to this rule is when a person's first name is compound, such as: Betty-Ann, Sue-Ellen, or Margaret Jane. Both names carry equal importance. Remember, it is essential to first set up the baptismal name to get the underlying traits, and then add the variations and changes.

NUMEROLOGY TELLS YOU HOW TO FULFILL
YOUR PURPOSE IN LIFE

Your total name tells what you must do to fulfill your purpose in life. It states the direction you must take. A father and son may have the same name, but they could not be alike, for their dates of birth differ. In the case of the suffix "senior" or any other one, or the prefix of "Doctor," they are omitted in calculations, just as we omit the prefixes of "Mr. and Mrs." which are not actually parts of their name. Twins having the same birthday will differ for several reasons:

1. Their names will vary.
2. Even though they were born on the same day, the hour and minutes would vary somewhat, which might affect the planet on the ascendant.

For your convenience, I will again set up the chart of numerological values for the letters in your name.

1.	A	J	S	
2.	B	K	T	
3.	C	L	U	
4.	D	M	V	11 reduces to 2
5.	E	N	W	22 reduces to 4
6.	F	O	X	33 reduces to 6
7.	G	P	Y	
8.	H	Q	Z	
9.	I	R	&	

EXAMPLES TO HELP YOU INTERPRET
YOUR NAME

Before you set up your own name and try to interpret it from the General Meaning given in Chapter 2, I'll set up several names as samples for you to follow in analyzing your own name. I would suggest that you again get out your pencil and scratch pad. Working with me will cement the steps in your mind more readily.

Patricia Neal, who won the academy award for the best actress several years ago, has a name total of 10 = 1, which is much stronger than a pure one (1). Let's look at her setup.

$$P\ A\ T\ R\ I\ C\ I\ A \qquad N\ E\ A\ L$$

$$\underline{7\ 1\ 2\ 9\ 9\ 3\ 9\ 1} \qquad \underline{5\ 5\ 1\ 3}$$

$$\frac{41}{5} \qquad\qquad \frac{14}{5}$$

$$5 + 5 = 10 = (1 + 0) = 1$$

Consulting the table, you should record the following: The P of Patricia = 7; A = 1; T = 2; R = 9; I = 9; C = 3; I = 9; A = 1. In the future I'll merely refer to the separate name totals, because you should be able to set up a name from the chart now. The total of the first name of Patricia is 41, a compound number, which if added together produces 5 because (4 + 1 = 5).

Using the same method, her last name of Neal reduces to 14, which if added together produces the single digit of 5. Now you add the subtotals, namely (5 + 5) = 10 to get the name total. This again reduces to 1 because (1 + 0 = 1), but you must remember that the reduced one comes from ten. There are two exceptions to this rule. They are numbers 11 and 22. Being master numbers, they are retained as such when occurring as a total. Otherwise they are reduced to a single digit, namely (11 = 2) and (22 = 4).

Patricia Neal's name total is one derived from ten. You will analyze or interpret it as follows:

> The one total indicates that she is an individualist (1), who had the courage (1) and determination (1) to overcome a severe illness which had left her crippled and speechless. Through perseverance (1) and will power (1) she has completely recovered, and is again performing on TV as an actress.

In the last chapter, when analyzing the nine, I mentioned that if anyone had many nines in his name, he could cope with any situation. The name of Patricia has three nines to help her. Now read what number one of the General Meaning on page 28 has to say about her.

Notice: For the present you should concentrate on figuring only the total name of yourself and the members of your family and friends. Later we will analyze each subtotal to learn how each name contributes to the total. Each name does have considerable influence on the interpretation of the full given name. Now see if you can write an interpretation, following the steps enumerated.

INSTRUCTIONS AND NINE STEPS
FOR YOU TO FOLLOW

Check your paper to see if you have included the following steps:

1. Record the full given name at birth.
2. Consult the table in Chapter 2 for the correct numerical value of each number.
3. Place each number directly under the appropriate letter.
4. Reduce each name separately to a single digit.
5. Retain all master totals of 11 and 22. Do not reduce these.
6. Add the subtotals to get the final total of the entire name.
7. Read what the table tells you about the number.
8. Later we'll read the explanation of each subtotal. Omit this for now.
9. Recheck all steps to be sure you have not forgotten something.

Another Sample for You to Work Is:

NAT KI NG COLE

<u>5 1 2</u> <u>2 9 5 7</u> <u>3 6 3 5</u>

8   <u>23</u>   <u>17</u>

8 + 5 + 8 = 21 = 3

The first name of Nat has a single total of 8. The middle name of King totals 23, which reduces to 5. The last name of Cole totals 17, which reduces to 8. The total name of Nat (8) plus King (5) plus Cole (8) = 21 = 3.

With a *three* as a whole name total, Nat King Cole had the talent to express himself well (3), in the entertainment field of music (3). He had a super imagination (1) and was creative in style, which gave him the opportunity to fill many engagements leading to his financial success (8). He had a good sense of humor (3), and he enjoyed social life (3).

Another Sample for You to Interpret Is:

MARGARET CHASE SMITH

<u>4 1 9 7 1 9 5 2</u> <u>3 8 1 1 5</u> <u>1 4 9 2 8</u>

<u>38</u>   <u>18</u   <u>24</u>
11   +   9   +   6   =

(11 + 15) = (11 + 6)

The first name of Margaret totals 38, which reduces to 11. The middle name of Chase totals 9. The last name of Smith totals 24, which reduces to 6. The total name of Margaret (11) plus Chase (9) plus Smith (6) = (11-15), which reduces to (11 + 6). There is an underlying 8 total, but we do not reduce the total to 8 because of the eleven in the total.

Margaret Chase Smith's total of (11 + 6) indicates she belongs in the limelight (11) in a civic capacity (6). As a United States Senator (11) in Washington (11) she represents the State of Maine (6). She should be an inspiration (11) for other women to follow in her footsteps and aspire to such a high office of service to her community (6). As a speaker (11) on various issues, she occupies the platform (11). She is diplomatic (11) in handling her constituents.

Now set up your own name and then try to write an interpretation for the number total of your full name. Be sure to follow the steps enumerated. Study the samples. I am confident you have learned some things about yourself you may not have known about before your analysis in numerology.

HOW TO DETERMINE THE ASPECTS OF EACH NUMBER

There are three aspects to each number. They are: (1) *The Constructive;* (2) *The Negative;* and (3) *The Destructive.*

There's an old saying to the effect that, "We chart your course, but you choose your aspects." This means that you are given certain numbers, but the disposition of them, as to whether you live constructively, negatively, or destructively is for you to decide, for the actual action or choice of results will be up to you.

Some numerologists refer to the constructive aspects as simply "positive." This can be ambiguous. A person can be "destructively" positive. Therefore, the term "positive constructive" or just "constructive" is better to use. Luckily, most individuals are making a sincere effort to live constructively. You may temporarily slide into a negative attitude of being critical or lazy, but if you curb these tendencies, they will not pull you down to be permanently destructive. The constructive vibration will create much peace of mind, health, and happiness.

WHAT IS A CONSTRUCTIVE MIND?

A constructive person makes an effort to be a leader or pioneer rather than a follower. He tries to build and not tear down. He makes an effort to succeed by his own will power.

WHAT IS A NEGATIVE MIND?

A negative individual is in the middle of a seasaw. He may be led up or down. He always follows the crowd, and does not contribute anything constructive to life. He lacks the courage to express himself.

WHAT IS A DESTRUCTIVE MIND?

A destructive individual never sees the bright side of anything. He is disagreeable, depressing, weakening, and pessimistic.

THE CONSTRUCTIVE ASPECTS OF NUMBERS

Number:

1. Activity, pioneering, independence, invention, force, ambition.
2. Diplomacy, cooperation, detail, harmony, service, rhythm.
3. Optimism, humor, joy, sociability, self-expression, enthusiasm.
4. Honesty, patience, economy, practicality, organization, loyalty.
5. Freedom, change, travel, adventure, progress, versatility.
6. Responsibility, musical talents, domesticity, service.
7. Silence, wisdom, research, study, introspection, spirituality.
8. Authority, leadership, management, executive ability.
9. Sympathy, philanthropy, universal love, artistic talent, service.
11. Intuition, inspiration, invention, revelation, idealism.
22. Practical idealist, power, internationalism, master builder.

THE NEGATIVE ASPECTS OF NUMBERS

Number:

1. Laziness, fear, instability, selfishness, obstinacy, braggadocio.
2. Carelessness, shyness, tactlessness, over-sensitivity; vacillation.
3. Gossip, pessimism, extravagance, repression, false pride.
4. Narrow-mindedness, rigidity, sterness, restriction.
5. Thoughtlessness, procrastination, irresponsibility, changeability.
6. Anxiety, worry, smugness, argumentativeness, meddlesome.
7. Sarcasm, melancholy, coldness, nervousness, humiliation.
8. Intolerance, impatience, strain, scheming, ruthlessness.
9. Emotionalism, selfishness, indiscretion, dissipation.
11. Shiftlessness, fanaticism, aimlessness, lack of understanding.
22. Inferiority complex, indifference, reproof, provincialism.

THE DESTRUCTIVE ASPECTS OF NUMBERS

Number:

1. Antagonism, tyranny, bigotry, domination, bully.
2. Cruelty, cowardice, anger, deception, passion.
3. Intolerance, jealousy, hypocrisy, deceit, avarice.
4. Hatred, vulgarity, violence, cruelty, jealousy, antagonism.
5. Sensuality, perversion, malevolence, debauchery, dope, drink.
6. Drudgery, cynicism, jealousy, conceit, domestic tyranny.
7. Dishonesty, suppression, faithlessness, malice.
8. Oppression, revenge, injustice, drink, artlessness.
9. Immorality, bitterness, falsehood, vice, dissipation, moroseness.
11. Dishonesty, miserly, wickedness, degradation, deterioration.
22. Wickedness, black magic, recklessness, impracticality, incapacity.

Notice: When figuring a name, it would simplify matters if you would confine your delineation of a name to its constructive aspects, as most people are making a sincere effort to try to live in a positive, constructive manner. However, if you find that the numbers seem to be incongruous, then it might be wise to look into the negative and destructive aspects. A criminal or rioter might show negative or destructive tendencies.

FOUR

How to Know Your
Secret Ambitions or Goals

Your heart's desire, soul's urge, or ideality is what you really want most out of life. It represents your secret ambition, ideal, goal, or aim, and it is the way your soul wishes to exprees itself for complete success. You can find it as your master guide by adding together the *vowels of your full name at birth* and reducing these to a single digit.

Notice: Numerologists may differ in what they call your inner self. Some may designate it as your heart's desire—others as your soul's urge—while still others may call it your secret ambition. Regardless of what term they may use, the meaning or interpretation is the same. Therefore, I have used the various names interchangeably so that you may become accustomed to whatever term, you may find. In summary, *your vowels tell what you desire to be, do, or have.*

WHAT THE VOWELS ARE

The vowels are: A, E, I, O, U, and sometimes Y. Y is a vowel when there is no other vowel in the syllable. *Example:* In the name of WYNN "y" is the vowel. "W" is never a first letter vowel. It is used only in combination with another vowel, and it follows the other vowel. An example of this is the "ew" in LEWIS. I do not use *W* as a vowel since its use is very limited.

HOW YOU CAN RECOGNIZE THE SECRET
OF YOUR VOWELS

Vowels are the backbone of our English language. Without vowels you could not pronounce words, for every syllable in the

English language has at least one vowel. They tell what you desire, and your way of looking at things. Vowels depict your inner self, or how you are deep inside—not how you appear to be when facing the general public—for no one can see inside of you to know how you think or feel. They show your inner strength.

HOW YOUR VOWELS REVEAL
SECRETS ABOUT YOURSELF

Numerology can reveal secrets by showing what your soul's urge, or that of another, is if you know the full name at birth. Even though you do not show your heart's desire, its secrets can be determined by interpreting the meaning of your vowels.

WHY YOU SHOULD LISTEN TO YOUR HEART'S
LONGING OR DESIRES

Your soul's urge indicates how you think, feel, and act. It reveals itself in the way your inner self strives for recognition. Your desire or goal will differ from the other members of your family because your beliefs vary. You, as well as every other individuals, believe you have a right to your own convictions.

The secret desires of some individuals are so strong that they will subordinate everything to achieve their goal. No obstacle is too great to hinder their progress. Other individuals will not listen to what their soul wants to tell them, and so they go through life with their desires unfulfilled. You should listen, through numerology for your heart wants to express your true character. All growth of your soul must come from within. It is the "HOW," or your motive for doing certain things.

EXAMPLES OF SETTING UP THE VOWELS

Now let's set up a name to illustrate the concept of vowels. I suggest you take your pencil and figure the numerology value of vowels with me for practice.

Final Value	6	$\dfrac{6}{15} = 3\ (6 + 6 = 12 = 3)$
Intermediate Count	6	

Vowel Count	5	1	9	5	1
Name:	E L L A		F I T Z G E R A L D		

The vowels of Ella are: E (5) and A (1) equals six. The vowels of Fitzgerald are: I (9) plus E (5) plus A (1) = 15 = 6. The total vowels of her name are Ella (6) plus Fitzgerald (6) equals twelve (12). One plus 2 = 3.

Step 1: Consult the table on page 17 for the numerical value of the vowels.
Step 2: Place the right number over each vowel. Total each name separately, and then together.
Step 3: Read the interpretation of each name.

Ella Fitzgerald's heart desire of three means she wants to express herself (3) as an entertainer (3). The subtotals of vowels in Ella (6) and Fitzgerald (6) indicate she is a singer (6) on the stage (6) or TV entertaining the family circle (6). She loves beauty and harmony (6). She is sympathetic (6), and wants to help others (6) by raising their standard of living. Sixes and threes indicate the artistic person who wants so express himself in music, writing, or acting. Now figure your own soul's urge by setting up your full name at birth. Place the correct numbers over the vowels of each name. Then add the vowels of each name separately, and then together to arrive at the total of all of her names. Consult the table or key on page 48 for your interpretation, depending on your particular subtotals and total.

Recently a friend was complaining about her husband. She said, "My husband and I quarrel constantly. I like to have fun at night, such as going to a dance or a show. He always insists on staying at home, either reading a book or watching television. Why can't we agree on doing the same thing?"

The reason they argue or disagree is that their soul's desires are inharmonious or dissimilar. She has a three heart's desire; his is a seven. This difference in their desires would cause constant friction between them. The only way they now can get along together, is for them to compromise by doing what she wants one time, and alternating with what he prefers to do. A *three* vowel total loves society, going to parties, and having a good time. A *seven* vowel total indicates a student or thinker, who likes to be alone, or spend his leisure hours at home quietly—either reading or studying.

If they had consulted a numerologist *before* their marriage, they would have been advised that they will never be compatible. A *three* and a *seven* will have conflicting desires, for they will want to travel in opposite directions, thus causing constant friction between themselves.

We'll set up one more sample and analyze it. *I would suggest that you figure this before looking at my interpretation, and then check it with mine.* Write out your analysis incorporating the meaning of the subtotals as well as the total.

Example:

Jackie Gleason's full given name at birth is: John Clarence Gleason.

$$6 \quad + \quad 11 \quad + \quad \frac{3}{12} = (11 - 9 = 11)$$

$\overline{6}$	$\overline{1 \; 5 \; 5}$	$\overline{5 \; 1 \; 6}$
J O H N	C L A R E N C E	G L E A S O N

$$\frac{6}{15} \quad + \quad \frac{3}{12} \quad = 9$$

$\overline{1 \qquad 9 \; 5}$	$\overline{5 \; 1 \quad 6}$
J A C K I E	G L E A S O N

As a comedian, (3) John Clarence Gleason wants to appear in the limelight (11) entertaining others (3) on TV (6) in the home (6) or community (6). He likes people (9), and wants to help others both financially as a humanitarian (9) and to lighten their burdens by making them laugh (3).

The vowels of his adopted name of Jackie Gleason total nine, which shows a desire to put the welfare of others above his own. He would rather be on the stage (3) entertaining others than do any other thing, for it is his whole life's interest. The nine total also includes acting or expressing himself in some creative way. While his original name is stronger than his adopted, the latter lends itself better to the footlights. The adopted carries the 3-6-9 trinity of the creative person, which is taken from the concords.

Now you are ready to check your delineation with mine. Perhaps you have even a more complete analysis than my synopsis.

VOWEL NUMEROLOGY TABLE OF YOUR HEART'S DESIRE OR SOUL'S URGE

Number 1 Characteristics

You:

Want to be independent to choose your own actions.
Have an urge to be creative and original.
Have a pioneering spirit, for you like to explore.
Have the ambition to be heard.
Want to be boss, for you have leadership qualities.
Desire intellectuality.
Are inclined to be selfish, critical, conceited, and arrogant.
Like to handle big affairs, and leave the details to others.
Are honest, loyal, and an instigator of action.
Number 1's lack patience, diplomacy, and tact, which they must cultivate.

Number 2 Characteristics

You:

Want harmony, peace, and truth.
Love music and the arts. You may be a speaker if the six is prominent.
Are refined and cultured.
Are very sensitive and emotional. Your feelings are easily hurt.
Prefer to follow rather than to lead.
Are diplomatic and tactful.
Are not fond of display, and prefer to be in the background.
Attract friends and society.
Like the opposite sex.
Are not a disciplinarian.
Are too easy going, and thus often become a doormat.
Are not ambitious for accomplishments.
Often are a student with psychic ability.
Number 2's need to cultivate a definite purpose in life.

Number 3 Characteristics

You:

Want self-expression in speaking, writing, or acting.
Love society, parties, and friends.
Are very ambitious, independent, and fearless.
Are a deep thinker, and can acquire knowledge easily.

Dislike detail, plodding, or staying in a rut.
Are intuitive and inspirational.
Are artistic, and have a good sense of color combinations.
Have a tendency to scatter your talents, as you are very versatile.
Love children and housepets.
Have a good sense of humor, and are a joy bringer.
Number 3's need to cultivate tolerance, patience, and concentration.
They must learn not to scatter their talents.

Number 4 Characteristics

You:

Are practical, analytical, and reliable.
Love loyalty and honesty.
Are patriotic.
Are a good disciplinarian.
Have determination and tenacity of purpose.
Have natural mechanical ability, and work well with your hands.
Are excellent in detail and routine work.
Have the ambition for material power.
Are rather narrow-minded in your viewpoint.
Want affection, but often fail to attract it due to your sternness.
Want order, for you are methodical and logical.
Are from Missouri and require proof.
No. 4's need to cultivate change, and be willing to accept the new while
   discarding the old.

Number 5 Characteristics

You:

Love change, adventure, travel, and new interests.
Are versatile and magnetic.
Are attracted to and liked by the opposite sex.
Are restless, nervous, and want freedom.
Have a quick mind, and are a good mixer.
Are philosophically inclined, and are investigative and promotive.
Are an adventurer at heart.
Dislike routine and detail.
Refuse to conform to conventional habits.
No. 5's must guard against a tendency to gamble and drink.
They must cultivate concentration, which they lack.

Number 6 Characteristics

You:

Love a home and family.
Want to be a cosmic teacher, parent, community worker, or nurse.
Love to give advice to others.
Want and need a home environment.
Enjoy working with others rather than alone.
Are responsible and domestically inclined.
Love the arts, harmony, and beauty.
Want to raise the standard of living.
Tend to be emotional.
Are sympathetic; want to help others but like appreciation.
Should have a good voice, either for speaking or singing.
No. 6's should guard against being argumentative, stubborn, or interfering with others.

Number 7 Characteristics

You:

Seek knowledge and wisdom above all things.
Want perfection.
Are introspective, studious, and theoretical.
Want the opportunity and quietude to meditate.
Are intuitive, inspirational, and sometimes retiring.
Love nature, i.e. the plants and animals.
Love mystery, and seek to understand spiritual laws.
Dislike noise and confusion.
Dislike manual labor and detail.
Are not popular in society, as you are seldom understood.
Are intellectual, scientific, philosophical, and spiritual.
No. 7's must learn to live alone and not be lonely.

Number 8 Characteristics

You:

Want to be a big business executive or leader.
Want to manage and direct, not follow.
Are intellectual, analytical, well-balanced, and efficient.
Have good judgment and a good sense of values.
Have tact, vision, and an imagination for good business success.
Want money and material power.
Are interested in expansion on a large scale.

Have strength, courage, and force.
No. 8's must learn organization and cooperation.
They sometimes lack the will power to forge ahead.

Number 9 Characteristics

You:

Want to be a humanitarian and philanthropist.
Would like to be a big brother to mankind.
Are generous and kind.
Are artistic, and want to share your knowledge with humanity.
Love travel and broad contacts.
Are attracted to and loved by everyone; you see the good in everyone.
Want to be a healer.
Give freely of yourself without expecting any reward.
Love music, the arts, and dramatics.
Your chief quality is universality and selfless love.
No. 9's must learn selflessness and service for the benefit of all.

Master Number 11 Characteristics

You:

Are intuitive, and want to be an inspiration to all.
Have psychic ability, and could be a seer.
Are religious and spiritual. You should follow your hunches.
Like to be inventive.
Are a universalist, forgetting the individual's needs.
Want to be a leader.
Must learn to mingle with the public, and give out knowledge for all.
No. 11's have the qualities listed under number 2, but in a greater
   degree.

Master Number 22 Characteristics

You:

Want to be a master builder on the material plane.
Are practical and theoretical.
Are a good diplomat, and would do well in governmental service.
Have high ideals and aspirations, and can master anything.
Have your feet firmly on the ground.
Have vision, are philosophical, but you are also logical.
No. 22's have the qualities of number four, but they are more dominant
   with higher ideals.

FIVE

How to Analyze Your Personality as Keyed to Consonants in Your Name

Your personality is your outer self, or the impression you make on others. People judge you by your appearance, namely, the care of your hair, nails, and clothing—your attitudes—your actions—and your voice. Personality should be the avenue through which your character, talents, and true self are expressed. Unfortunately this is not always the case, for it often serves as a cover-up of your inner self, which may be weak and even lack sincerity. An honest and a well-balanced personality is as much a credit to an individual as is a huge bank account, for it is a means of success and achievement.

WHAT THE CONSONANTS IN YOUR NAME MEAN

The sum of all of the consonants of your original full name at birth is your *personality* or *appearance* number. Consonants constitute the letters remaining after the vowels A, E, I, O, U, and sometimes Y have been removed. *Remember, your personality is what others think you are from the impression you make on them.*

HOW YOU CAN CHANGE YOUR PERSONALITY

A composite of many things makes up your personality, just as a cake has many ingredients. Luckily, if you are dissatisfied with yourself, you can change your personality, for it is the actor playing to his audience. You can alter or improve your personality by changing your attitude, actions, thoughts, words, and appearance. In judging others, since their personalities may be deceiving, you should also look at the inner self or soul's urge before you make a decision about them.

The Case of Mary A

When Mary A came to see me, she seemed to be quite puzzled about the attitude and actions of her husband Bill. She said that while Bill was courting her, he had a captivating personality. This attracted everyone including herself. He was always smiling and complimenting her on her appearance. He seemed to be pleased with everything she did or said. Now that they are married, he still is polite to her. He has all of the admirable traits he formerly had but, she added, "that just about describes him. We have nothing in common. He spends all of his spare time either working cross-word puzzles or reading comic books. When I turn on the television to listen to a serious program, news broadcast, or a drama, he quickly jumps up from his chair and asks if it's agreeable with me to change the station to a variety show. He never can be pinned down to a serious conversation. Why has he changed so much?"

When I quickly set up his chart and skimmed over the highlights, I found that his personality number of *eleven* was much greater than his heart's desire number of *five*. He had not changed since their marriage. She had been so fascinated before their marriage by the good impression he made with his *eleven* personality, that she failed to realize that he could not live up to what he pretended to be *because he lacked a strong heart's desire*. If the heart's desire of a person is as strong or even stronger than the personality, then that individual will be worth cultivating, for he will be all that he appears to be and perhaps even more so. If the personality is stronger than the soul's urge, namely, an *eleven personality* and a *five heart's desire*, he may appeal to you at first, but eventually he may prove to be a huge disappointment. He may tarnish on the long run acquaintance basis, or fall short of what is expected of him, and not grow in interest on further association with him.

SETTING UP A NAME WITH CONSONANTS

I'll now set up a name to illustrate the use of the consonants.

Step 1: Turn to the chart on page 17 to determine the numerical value of each consonant.

Step 2: Place the appropriate number under each consonant.

Step 3: Add the consonants of each name separately and reduce them to a single digit for subtotals.

Step 4: Add the total digit of the consonants of each name to get a name total of consonants.

Step 5: Turn to the table on page 55 to read the interpretation.

An Analysis of Mr. Colby (illustrative case)

Here's how Mr. Colby would set up for consonant analysis:

$$\text{J A M E S} \quad \text{A L L E N} \quad \text{C O L B Y}$$

$$\underline{1 \quad 4 \quad 1} \quad \underline{\quad 3 \; 3 \quad 5} \quad \underline{3 \quad 3 \; 2 \; 7} = (11 + 3) \text{ Personality}$$

$$6 \quad + \quad 11 \quad \quad \underline{15}$$

$$6 = 23 = 5$$

The consonants of James are: J = 1; M = 4; S = 1, totalling six. The consonants of Allen are: L = 3; L = 3; N = 5, totalling eleven. The consonants of Colby are: C = 3; L = 3; B = 2; Y = 7, totalling 15 = 1 + 5 = six. The total consonants are (11 + 6 + 6) or 11 + 3, because 6 + 6 = 12 = 3. While the underlying single digit of five constitutes the personality, reduced, you must realize it is made up of (11 + 3), which is much stronger than a plain five. When the master number eleven occurs in the total we do not reduce it, but we carry it out as a subtotal to show what underlies the five.

To find how James Allen Colby appears to others, turn to Number *five* in the table of personality. To help you, I'll enumerate the highlights.

James Allen Colby has a scintillating personality (11-3). He is liked by both sexes (5). He can express himself well (3), in an illuminating (11) manner, which captivates his audience (6) and puts him on the platform (11) or limelight. He will be well dressed and make a youthful appearance (5). He should be a good conversationalist (6).

Now get your pencil and paper and we'll set up another name. After you have figured the chart of Alexander Graham Bell, inventor of the telephone, check to see if you agree with my delineation.

ALEXANDER GRAHAM BELL

3	6	5 4	9	7 9	8	4	2	3 3

$$27 \qquad\qquad 28 \qquad\qquad 8$$

$$9 \qquad\qquad \underline{10} \qquad\qquad 8$$

$$1$$

$$9 \quad + \quad 1 \quad + \quad 8 = 18 = 9$$

Alexander Graham Bell has a personality number of *nine*, made up of subtotals of Alexander (9), plus Graham (1) plus Bell (8). He is all that he appears to be with a vowel total of ten, showing a desire to be original and do something in the pioneering line (1) independently, for the sake of helping others (9). His personality of nine is not greater than his heart's desire number of ten, indicating that he can live up to his appearance or the impression he makes. Others judge him to be a person interested in some line of business (8) which will benefit others (9) in an original (1) way. He lived up to expectations, for he served others by inventing the wireless which has been a great step in the progress of mankind.

Now set up your own chart and learn what is your personality number. Then write an interpretation of your own personality by not only analyzing the total but also the subtotals of your separate names and blending them with the whole.

TABLE OF PERSONALITY CONSONANT NUMBERS

Number 1 Characteristics

You:

Will appear to others as donimant, forceful, and creative.
Should wear distinctive clothing which is unusual, such as stripes or plaids.
Should look dignified but correct in line and details.
Should wear and furnish your home in clear, bright colors.
Should strive not to be overweight.

Number 2 Characteristics

You:

Should always be neat and clean.
Have a pleasing, agreeable manner.

Are peaceful, quiet, and diplomatic.
Must cultivate a flair for wearing clothes.
Should wear soft, flowing materials, not loud colors.
Should avoid being colorless and too plain.
Should wear neutral colors, for they are appropriate for you.
Are loved, modest, and you seek to be cooperative.

Number 3 Characteristics

You:

Should wear attractive clothing and be very fashionable.
Are friendly and sociable.
Should add accessories of frills, ribbons, or bows to your attire.
Must watch wearing too extreme styles and overdressing.
Should choose distinctive jewelry, for you have a flair for the unusual.
Should enjoy beauty and comfort.
Look well in almost any style and color.

Number 4 Characteristics

You:

Look well in tailored clothing with straight lines.
Are precise and plain, but interesting.
Are practical, conservative, dependable, and orderly.
May have square shoulders, and may be inclined to be heavyset.

Number 5 Characteristics

You:

Are a leader of fashions. You are versatile and up-to-date.
Often go to extremes, such as wearing furs in July.
Should avoid being flashy.
Are always youthful in appearance.
Have a magnetic and interesting personality.
Like and are liked by the opposite sex.
Have a sense of humor, and are an excellent conversationalist.

Number 6 Characteristics

You:

Are neat, attractive, and charming.
Are the motherly type in appearance. You should be well dressed.
Are not as stylish as a number three or a number five.

Like to be comfortable. Therefore, you often choose loose and easy to wear clothing.
Are sympathetic, and draw others to you for advice and comfort.
Are interested in a home and family.
Should avoid being overweight.
Create an atmosphere of harmony and responsibility.

Number 7 Characteristics

You:

Are well-groomed and often wear expensive material.
Are somewhat aloof, reserved, and exclusive.
Should wear straight lines with accents of color in jewelry.
Have a distinctive, perfected personality.
Should wear pastels.

Number 8 Characteristics

You:

Should look influential and successful even though you are penniless.
Like good materials, such as tweeds and plaids.
Prefer tailor-made clothing or sports wear.
Like to give the impression of wealth. You dislike cheap things.
Are friendly, persuasive, and dominant in manner.
Are careful of details such as your shoes, ties, and handkerchiefs.

Number 9 Characteristics

You:

Are generous, friendly, and a good fellow.
Have a magnetic personality, but sometimes you lack force.
Are a big brother to all.
Are romantic, charming, and sympathetic.
Should use and wear colors, avoiding black.
Should watch carelessness in dress, for you like to be comfortable.

Number 11 Characteristics

You:

Are often a dreamer with your head in the clouds.
Are idealistic and inspirational.
Are individualistic in dress and action.
Are often intuitive, and have a spiritual side to your nature.
Should wear smooth materials of fine texture.

Number 22 Characteristics

You:

Should always wear expensive looking clothing with straight lines.
Give the appearance of being a master builder or expert in any field.
Are cooperative and generous in actions to impress the public.
Have your feet on the ground, and you are very practical.
Always appear wealthy, even though you may be broke.

SIX

How to Find Your Destiny or Expression Numbers

You were born for a definite purpose in life. What your mission is can be reavealed by your destiny or expression number. It states what you must do or be in this particular life span to be successful in every phase of your life.

HOW YOU CAN FIND YOUR DESTINY NUMBER

Your destiny number can be found by adding together all of the letters of your full given name at birth and reducing these to a single digit. It suggests the type of individuals you should gather around you and associate and work with—what you should contribute to others in the way of help and work—and your field or source of opportunity for success.

IT'S NOT ALWAYS EASY TO FULFILL
YOUR PURPOSE IN LIFE

It is not always an easy or a simple matter to fulfill the requirements of your destiny or expression number. You might want to do something entirely different from what you should experience, but eventually, if you make a sincere effort to strive in the direction of your destiny, avenues will be open for you, and you will succeed in accomplishing your purpose. Your reason for existence is revealed by your destiny number.

A CASE IN POINT WHY NUMEROLOGY IS
NOT FORTUNE-TELLING

Recently I had a call from a girl saying she had been engaged to a man for two years. Every time she even suggested setting a date for the wedding, he found some excuse for delaying the event. Her question was: "Will he ever decide it's the right time to get married, or will he continue to postpone the date?" She told me their full dates of birth and their full given names.

Since he has a destiny number of seven and a pinnacle number of nine (see Chapter Eleven), I doubt if he will ever reach the decision to marry her or anyone. The seven destiny indicates a person who enjoys his own company best. He prefers to study and analyze situations and be alone a great deal of the time. With the nine pinnacle he may experience many disappointments and losses, at least for the duration of the nine pinnacle. It is an ending period and not one in which to begin a marriage. She had both a six destiny and a six pinnacle number. A person with a six destiny should marry and have the responsibilities of a home and a family. She is sure to experience the love and home vibration with a six pinnacle. Therefore, I suggested to her that she start looking around for greener pastures. Her numbers strongly indicate she will meet another man with serious intentions, if she decides to break the perennial engagement with her fiance.

You can see from the above delineation that numerology is based on facts arrived at through numbers, and is not fortune-telling.

YOU ARE EQUIPPED FOR SUCCESS

Your destiny may be entirely different from that of your neighbor. Luckily, you were equipped at birth with all of the tools necessary to accomplish some special mission, which you can do better than any other person, but you alone can and must start the ball rolling for your success.

When you work at a job, whether it is of the white-collared variety, or one involving manual labor, you must learn to meet the obligations or requirements well, in order to be promoted even one step for a higher job on the scale. If you procrastinate, you will remain at the same level, or you may be demoted, or even "fired."

YOU HAVE AN EQUAL CHANCE WITH EVERYONE ELSE

While on the surface it may not look as though you have an equal chance with others, actually you do have. This doesn't mean that you can do, and will have the opportunity to tackle the other fellow's job, but you do have the tools to dig and do your own special task.

YOUR OPPORTUNITY FOR SUCCESS

It is more important to know your destiny or expression number than any other number in your numerological chart, because it tells you specifically what you must do or be, and not what you are or may desire to be or to accomplish.

Your destiny number gives your opportunity for success, and what part you are to play, as long as you fulfill the divine or definite purpose revealed by the total letters of your given name at birth.

When you realize you are working out your destiny for your soul's experience, then you will know troubles are necessary if you expect to be promoted and grow spiritually as a well-rounded person able to meet any situation successfully.

HOW TO DETERMINE YOUR MISSION IN LIFE

Some of you are born to serve, some to entertain and be joy bringers, some to be peacemakers, and still others to be financial geniuses. What your mission in life should be is no secret for anyone who can analyze and unravel the meaning behind the *destiny number.* Even if you never use your full given name at birth, or if you change your name entirely, its effects will still be felt and remain your soul's true destiny.

Your nickname, changes in signature, and your married name all contribute to, and are avenues through which your destiny is fulfilling the purpose of your life.

HOW TO ARRIVE AT YOUR DESTINY NUMBER

Up to the present time you learned in this book to set up a full given name and analyze only the total name or number. Also you learned how to set up your vowels or heart's desire, or your

personality (consonants) separately. Now you will utilize what
you have learned in previous chapters by:

Step 1: Setting up the full given name at birth.

Step 2: Figuring the soul's urge and reducing this to a single digit.

Step 3: Figuring the personality and reducing this to a single total.

Step 4: Analyzing the sub-totals of all single digits in addition to their totals, in order to get a more comprehensive understanding of each total.

**SETTING UP THE NAME OF
JOHN FITZGERALD KENNEDY**

Now we'll set up a name to illustrate the above steps and arrive
at the destiny number.

$$= (1 + 3) = 4 \text{ Soul's urge}$$

Total Vowel Count	6	+	6	+				1 = 13		
			15					10		
Vowel Count	6		9	5	1			5	5	
NAME	J O H N		F I T Z G E R A L D					K E N N E D Y		
Consonant Count	1 8 5		6 2 8 7 9 3 4					2 5 5 4 7		
	14		39					23		
	5		12					5		
(personality)	5	+	3	+				5 = 13 = 4		
(destiny)	11	+	9	+				6 = (11 + 6		
								8		

First add the vowels of John (6) plus Fitzgerald (6) plus
Kennedy (1) = 13 = 4. Then add the consonants of John (5) plus

Fitzgerald (3) plus Kennedy (5) = 13 = 4. Now add the vowels of John and his consonants together, namely 6 + 5 = 11. Then add the vowels and consonants of Fitzgerald together, namely, 6 + 3 = 9. Then add the vowels and consonants of Kennedy in the same way, namely, 1 + 5 = 6. Now add the totals together, namely, 11 + 9 + 6 = (11 + 6) (8 reduced).

We add each name separately before arriving at a total of all the names because each name has a definite effect on how the destiny will be carried out. We never add the vowels and consonants together to arrive at a destiny number, for as JFK's case proves, we may lose an *eleven* or a *twenty-two*. If we had added the vowel and consonant totals together merely, we would have lost the *eleven* total of John, which makes his destiny stronger than a pure *eight* i.e. (11+6), although the underlying number is still *eight*. Also, credit for master numbers may be given an individual when he actually does not show the master number in the total. An example of this would be by adding the vowel and consonant totals and arriving at an *eleven* when if added separately the total would have been twenty.

WHAT J.F.K.'S DESTINY NUMBER TELLS ABOUT HIM

John Fitzgerald Kennedy's destiny number of *(11 + 6)* indicates that his purpose in life was to appear in the limelight (11) before the public (4) in an inspirational capacity (11) by holding down a responsible (6) position in some civic (6) field, serving the community or his country. His vowel total of *four,* made up of 6-6-1 states that his main desire was to appear before crowds (4) in a governmental or political (4) capacity. He wanted to be practical and be down-to-earth. Whether he accomplished his desire depends greatly on how hard he worked for his purpose, and not on wishes or desires only.

His personality number of *four* was the same as his soul's urge or ambition number of *four*. This indicates he was all that he appeared to be, no more and no less. His personality number of *four* is made up of 5-3-5, which shows he was youthful (5) in appearance and actions, liked by both sexes (5), and had a jovial (3) disposition. He was well able to express himself (3). He also enjoyed society and having fun.

The underlying eight of his destiny total suggests that his purpose in life was to conduct a large corporation or big business (8). As President of the United States, he fulfilled his mission in

life (11-6 = 8) through super diplomacy (11), dealing with people
(9), and rendering service (6).

WHAT EACH OF YOUR NAMES SIGNIFY

Your first or given name is the personal or individual side of
your nature. The middle or second name acts as a reserve or well
from which you may draw assets if necessary, and the last or the
hereditary name indicates your family characteristics, usually on
your father's side, with its strengths and weaknesses. All together
the names designate talents and traits, and state what you must
do. You can never outlive your requirements. When you understand what your expression should be, you will sincerely try to
perform your job. Then the task will become easier, and eventually you will succeed in accomplishing your purpose or reason
for being born.

We will now set up the name of Richard Milhaus Nixon,
President of the United States, and figure his destiny. Be sure to
follow the four steps given previously in this chapter.

$$
\begin{array}{ccccccc}
1 & + & 4 & + & 6 & = 11 & \text{(vowels)} \\
\underline{10} & & \underline{13} & & \underline{15} & & \\
9 \quad 1 & & 9 \quad 1\,3 & & 9 \quad 6 & &
\end{array}
$$

RI CHARD   MI LHAUS   NI XON

$$
\begin{array}{ccc}
9 \quad 38 \quad 94 & 4 \quad 38 \quad 1 & 5 \quad 6 \quad 5 \\
\underline{33} & \underline{16} & \underline{16} \\
6 \quad\quad + & 7 \quad\quad + & 7 = \quad \underline{20} \ \text{(consonant)} \\
7 \quad\quad + & 11 \quad\quad + & 4 = (11 + 11) = 22 \ \text{(destiny)}
\end{array}
$$

First add the vowels of Richard (1), plus Milhaus (4), plus Nixon
(6) = 11. Add the consonants of Richard (6), plus Milhaus (7) plus
Nixon (7) = 20. Total of Richard is 7, plus Milhaus 11, plus Nixon
4 = (11 + 11) = 22.

President Nixon's destiny number of a pure twenty-two, is the
greatest master destiny possible. It is made up of two elevens

(limelight), which are also master numbers, but they add up to a single total of twenty-two. The twenty-two gives him both national and international influence. His soul's urge of eleven total is made up of subtotals of 6-4-1, indicating a deep desire to appear on the platform (11) in an inspirational manner (11), before the public (4). With the master number of eleven total vowels he wants to be an inspiration to others and a leader in the capacity of serving and helping his fellowman through civic or governmental work (4).

His consonant total of twenty, made up of 6-7-7, shows him to be very sensitive (2) to criticism (7). His consonant total of twenty would amount to the same as the vowel total of eleven if we reduced this to two, which shows that he not only is all he appears to be but more, for it actually is eleven, a master number. He is quiet (2), dignified (2), inspirational, and analytical (7). His aim is to be a peacemaker (20). The twenty consonant total is ten times stronger than a pure two. With the two sevens, he has an excellent mind to analyze problems and to think them out to a conclusion, for he has much knowledge. He can probe into conditions both of national and international scope.

With so many master numbers, President Nixon is well-qualified for the high position he holds. Whether he lives up to the full potentials of his super numbers will be interesting to watch, but he has all the qualities to be a great president.

WHAT TO DO IF A CHILD IS ADOPTED

If a child has been adopted and you know his original name, then the latter name should be used, as it gives his real destiny. If a person legally changes his name, the same principle holds true of using the given name at birth, while the changes in signature and spelling give added tools for accomplishments.

TABLE OF DESTINY OR EXPRESSION NUMBERS

Number 1 Characteristics

Your mission in life is to be a leader, pioneer, or the head of a business, but success will only come through your own efforts by exerting initiative, independence, and originality. You must develop will power, learn to think for yourself, be self-reliant, and be determined to be self-made and succeed through your own ability. Be constructive in thought, and don't be afraid to be different, individualistic, or investigate new ideas. If you must deal in an old established firm, try to inject new and original methods. While you should be a leader and a promoter, this doesn't mean you should be dictatorial, domineering, or too aggressive. It means to meet obstacles with courage.

Number 2 Characteristics

You were meant to be a diplomat or peacemaker. You can harmonize conditions, and gain cooperation by your tact, magical power of attraction, and by arbitration, for you have the ability to see both sides of an issue. While not a leader, you have the patience to be a collector, and to handle details. You can be a statistician, for compiling material for future expression or use is your stock in trade. You may be called upon constantly to settle disputes. A partnership is a better approach for you than independently owning your own business. Marriage is advisable, as well as joining clubs, for this will give you an opportunity to cooperate and share with others. You should cultivate the arts such as music, dancing, singing, or painting, for you have a good sense of rhythm, timing, and color.

Number 3 Characteristics

You were destined for self-expression in words either in writing, acting, or speaking. Entertaining others, you were meant to be a joy bringer. Your job is to arouse spirit and imagination so that others will learn how to laugh. You will be popular, loved, and acquire money. You should be creative, inspirational, and artistic. You should be optimistic, active, helpful, and a true friend. Since you have a gift of words, you should be interested in the theatre, opera, literature, writing, and speaking or acting.

Number 4 Characteristics

You were meant to be a builder. You are a hard worker and honest, with your feet placed squarely on the ground. You would make a good office manager as you are conscientious, reliable, economical, and excellent in detail and routine. You could succeed as a efficiency expert, for you are analytical, systematic, and orderly. You can assume much responsibility and help to protect others. You are practical, sincere, and determined.

Number 5 Characteristics

Your destiny points toward the lighter side of life. You will have freedom and liberty. You should willingly accept new ideas, change, new methods, and progress. Be versatile, clever, and courageous. You will have many experiences. Use them for growth. You will like social life and the opposite sex. You should excel in selling, advertising, promoting new ideas or thoughts, travel, and in public relations.

Number 6 Characteristics

Your mission in life is service, both in the home and in the community, for six is a love vibration centered around the family. You are a cosmic parent or teacher. You are loving and sympathetic, and you can assume much responsibility. You would make a good musician for rhythm, harmony, and beauty are a way of life for you. A home life is essential for your happiness. You should serve humanity as a nurse, doctor, teacher, musician, actor, or horticulturist. You might also be attracted to and succeed as a farmer, florist, rancher, engineer, interior decorator, or welfare worker. You could succeed in the theatre as a performer, for you should have a good voice.

Number 7 Characteristics

You were meant to be an educator in the field of science or the mysteries of life. You are a deep thinker, and could succeed in inventive and scientific pursuits, as well as uncovering the hidden meaning of nature. You need to spend some time alone and in silence in order to meditate and receive inspiration from within. You should be a specialist and live by realities and not by superficialities. You are inclined to gather knowledge from all sources. Partnerships, including marriage, may not be successful for you. Gaining understanding and acquiring wisdom should be your aim. You could do research work, study religion, or be a writer, lawyer, technician, or an expert on antiques. You must be discriminating, gathering facts, and weighing them carefully before imparting your findings to others. You may be considered strange or out of the ordinary, since you are a loner and follow the unusual path. You may be sought as a counselor due to your superior knowledge.

Number 8 Characteristics

Your life is destined for big business and finance. You can make money, but this should not be your ultimate aim. You must learn to recognize the balance between the material and the spiritual forces. Success will come only through your own efforts, not through luck. Justice should be your watchword. You shouldn't waste time striving for a fortune, but work for personal satisfaction and accomplishment. Your reward should be seeing a task well done. You may be interested in sports and general entertainment. Take an interest in government and civic affairs. Publishing, printing, and manufacturing are open fields for you as well as banking, or being the head of a business. You should associate vith influential and talented people. You may be philosophically and religiously inclined.

Number 9 Characteristics

You were intended to be a big brother to humanity expressing love, compassion, and understanding. Service is your duty. You must learn to be impersonal. To lean too much on personal love and possessions may be disappointing, for you may lose them. To give is to receive for a nine destiny. Life is beautiful, and there are many opportunities open for you to help others. You could be a teacher, writer, actor, doctor, nurse, lawyer, or a philanthropist. Doing social work would also be a wide-open field for you.

Number 11 Characteristics

Consult number two (2) for its lesser qualities, but if you are living positively, eleven is original, intuitive, and a master leader along spiritual and inspirational lines. You belong in the limelight before the public. You are an idealist and could be a leader, teacher, philosopher, or a psychologist. Dealing in electricity, aviation, invention, television, and radio are harmonious occupations for you. You may be a religious writer or minister. If you fail to live up to the opportunities offered by your destiny number, you may revert to being a two, which will find you more restricted. Two deals in details and routine work. You may also find yourself becoming a doormat.

Number 22 Characteristics

Consult number four (4) for its lesser possibilities, but the master number twenty-two (22), if living constructively, can be a universal master of international fame. Number twenty-two is a master builder on the material plane. You should work with large groups. You could aspire to being the head of a big institution, an ambassador, a diplomat, buyer, builder, organizer, statesman, or an efficiency expert. A twenty-two who fails to live up to his capabilities becomes a limiting four, engaged in the occupation of a clerk, an accountant, a farmer, foreman, or a governmental employee such as civil service worker.

SEVEN

Your Birthpath

WHAT TALENTS YOU BROUGHT WITH YOU AT BIRTH

In learning your life's lesson, you may suffer many disappointments and setbacks, but if you continue to persist in your effort, you are bound to pass the grade. The manner in which you can easily conquer your obligation or learn your lesson is stated in your *birthpath*.

WHAT YOUR NUMEROLOGICAL REPORT CARD TELLS YOU

Your total birthpath consists of the sum of your month, day, and year of your birth. It is your report card or bank account stating what lessons you have learned in past lives, and what you brought with you at the time of your birth in the way of assets, such as your talents, character, and ability to meet the experiences of your present destiny.

HOW TO CHOOSE YOUR RIGHT VOCATION

The sum of the day, month, and year of your birth specifies the grade you are now in, in the school of life. It gives the clue to your vocational tendencies and possibilities. It tells the job you are best fitted to do. When you know what your ability is, then it should be relatively easy for you to fulfill the requirements of your destiny. Your birthpath states what you have to your credit—not what you must do.

YOUR NUMEROLOGICAL GRADE IN THE SCHOOL
OF LIFE

When you entered the eighth grade in the beginning of the school year in September, you may not have known the answers to questions asked concerning the subjects to be studied, nor did you know how to solve the required mathematical problems, but you did have background knowledge of the previous seven grades to help you learn the lessons of the eighth grade. (At the end of the school year, you should have had the general knowledge expected of that grade. If you did not, you failed to be promoted.)

In the school of life the same principle is true. The grade you are in (found from your total numerological birthpath), will be difficult until you have made a sincere effort to fulfill its requirements. When this is accomplished, it will be an asset, and it will then work for your advancement.

WHY YOU ARE SOMETHING SPECIAL

No two people in the universe are exactly alike. A father and a son may have the same name, but their year of birth could not be identical. Twins born on the same day differ, even identical twins, for they could not have the same name. Names, when spoken, emit definite and individual vibrations. Even if two individuals had the same name and date of birth, their first or nicknames would vary. This would eliminate them from being of the Siamese variety.

HOW TO LEARN WHAT YOUR TALENTS ARE

In analyzing your birthday, you will learn what talents you possess to carry out your vocation or total birthpath. You can't change the day on which you were born. While it is possible to change your name, although the original name always remains in the background and demands attention, your birthdate is constant—it never changes.

To figure your birthpath or vocation, you simply add the day, month, and year of your birth together. If the result is a compound number, you again reduce this to a single digit.

Example:

If your total birthpath, is twenty-three (a compound number), you would then reduce this to a single digit by adding (2 + 3 = 5), for the final birthpath number of five. This is the same procedure we have been following in previous chapters.

HOW TO FIND THE NUMBER OF YOUR MONTH OF BIRTH

In determining the numerical value of the month in which you were born, you simply follow the calendar sequence to arrive at the number attributed to each month.

For Example:

January	=	1	July	=	7
February	=	2	August	=	8
March	=	3	September	=	9
April	=	4	October	=	10
May	=	5	November	=	11
June	=	6	December	=	12

To demonstrate how you should set up your own birthpath and analyze it, we'll use as an example the name of John David Rockefeller. Follow the explanation closely so that you can figure the next example yourself.

John David Rockefeller was born on July 8, 1839. His birthpath number was nine (9).

Example:

JULY	8	1839	=	9	(birthpath)
7	8	21			
		3			

Analysis:

$$7 \; + \; 8 \; + \; 3 = 18 \; = (1+8=9)$$

July, the month of his birth, is the seventh month. His birthday is the single digit of eight (showing his talents). The year of his birth (1839) added together produces three.

Namely:

$$(1+8+3+9) = 21 = (2+1) = 3$$

Mr. Rockefeller's birthpath of nine was made up of the month (7), plus the day (8), plus the year (3) totalling nine reduced. His birthday on the eighth indicates he had the ability to be a big business executive (8). He was practical and down to earth (8). He examined conditions or problems thoroughly (7), for he was a perfectionist, before deciding on a big business venture (8). Luckily he had creative ability (3) to express himself well before people (9). With a nine birthpath, he had to learn to be a big brother to humanity (9), serving them before gratifying his own desires. He mixed creative (3), scientific (7), and business acumen (8) in a melting pot to produce a financial success, and a philanthropist (9) of wide renown (9).

Many people born with a nine birthpath are self-centered. They may suffer many disappointments or losses until they learn to first serve others, and work for the betterment of all. If they have learned their lesson, then the tide will turn, and success will be their reward in whatever field they concentrate upon following.

Now get your pencil and paper and be ready to figure the next birthpath. After completing it, check to see if you agree with me.

Example:

Ed Sullivan was born on September 28, 1901. He is known as "Mr. T.V."

SEPTEMBER	28	1901	=	(11 + 10)	Birthpath
9	10	11			

$$9 \; + \; 1 \; + \; 11 = \quad (11+10) = 3, \text{ as we reduce it,}$$
$$(1+0) \qquad\qquad (21) \qquad\qquad (2+1)$$

Mr. Sullivan's birthpath of 11 + 10 arrived at by adding his month (9) plus day (1) plus year (11) indicates that it was necessary for him to learn to express himself (3) on the platform (11) in an original (10) capacity. His birthday of (28-10-1) tells you that he has the talent of a super-individualist or salesman (1), who does things in a creative manner (10). His TV show has surpassed any other from the standpoint of the length of time it has been on the air, which is over twenty years. His subtotals of month (9), plus day (1) plus year (11) indicate that his appeal is to the many (9), for most people like his variety show. It is illuminating (11) and original (10) in content, at least it was when it started many years ago. He has helped many newcomers (10) "crash" the entertainment field (3) by giving them a chance to perform (9) on his program in various fields.

Now set up your own birthpath, using the month, day and year of your birth. Reduce this to a single total. Consult the table on page 74 for the interpretation, depending on your total final digit analysis. Be deliberate, and tie your conclusions together to form the whole picture as developed from the tables as indicated by the examples set out in this chapter for you.

Following are the characterictics or significance of the numbers in the birthpath as developed in this chapter.

COMPLETE INTERPRETATION OF BIRTHPATH NUMBERS AND THEIR SIGNIFICANCE

Number 1-Independence

You must learn to be a pioneer, and have no hesitancy in tackling the unusual or original. You should be creative, inventing new things. Since you neither work well under the direction of others, nor do you like to take orders, you should be at the head of a business. You are an individualist in thought and action. You must develop executive ability, will power, and a broad vision, so that you may succeed as a manager of a department store or as a foreman. Other fields open to you are selling, engineering, aviation, writing, speaking, engineering, automotive line, or sales promotion activities. You are often born in a family where you are forced to be dependent. Negative qualities which you should guard against are: being headstrong and bossy, set in habits, egotistical, overconfident, selfish, and impatient with others. New and original ideas and methods are your assets.

Number 2—Cooperation

You must develop tact and diplomacy. Your appeal should be to groups and communities, for you must learn to be a good mixer, gentle, and persuasive. Your success depends greatly upon helping others without expecting any reward. You are a natural peacemaker and arbitrator. You can succeed well in governmental work or politics. Other successful lines for you are music, painting, and dancing, for you have a good sense of rhythm and timing. You must learn to be good at detail work. You could also be an excellent librarian, secretary, auditor, teller, or statistician. Negative qualities are: you are too sensitive and timid. Instead of being courageous, you are often afraid of making a mistake. You may be born in a garrulous family in which you must settle disputes.

Number 3—Self-Expression

You must learn to express yourself well, for you have a gift for using words in writing, speaking, and acting. You should be creative, for you have a good imagination. You possess intuitive qualities, and should succeed best in mental work. Having an excellent sense of humor, you should mingle with others socially. Being very versatile and capable, you are apt to scatter your talents, which may keep you from achieving outstanding success. You should learn to follow your hunches. You may succeed as a writer, public speaker, critic, minister, artist, advertiser, actor, lawyer, beauty operator, health and food expert, interior decorator, and in psychic endeavors. You should guard against being critical of others, impatient, intolerant, and overly optimistic. You may be born in a family where you are repressed and forced to do detail, routine, or manual labor, which will prevent you from using your initiative and creative talents.

Number 4—Organization

You must learn to be practical, down-to-earth, dependable, and conservative. You must learn to take orders, for you should demand as much from yourself as from others. You are quite set in your ways. Because you concentrate too much on details, you often neglect taking advantage of bigger things. You could succeed well as an architect, farmer, contractor, technician, mechanic, tailor, draftsman, electrician, teacher, bookkeeper, accountant, domestic, or owning or running a small business. Dealing in commodites is another field in which you could be successful.

Number 5–Freedom

You should learn to be versatile, for you ought to pursue more than one line of endeavor at the same time. You should want to be free to travel, try new things, make changes, and follow the unusual paths. Your appeal is to both sexes and to crowds. You will never settle down willingly to routine work. You must be careful not to indulge in the vices of drink, sex, and dope, for you could easily fall a prey to wasting your talents. You have much vitality and enthusiasm, and will remain the eternal youth. Aspects to avoid are being restless, discontented, and wanting constant change. You must learn to stick to a task until it is completed. You may succeed as a traveling salesman, advertiser, diagnostician, psychologist, writer, personnel director, detective, teacher, promoter, druggist, teacher of the occult, lecturer, or as a writer of mystery or detective stories.

Number 6–Service

You must learn to succeed well in any endeavor pertaining to education, the home, or the family. Some fields open for you are nursing, teaching, cooking, heading an institution, social worker, principal of a school, parent, hospital worker, minister, dealer in foods, welfare worker, dressmaker, milliner, interior decorator, artist, musician, farmer, furniture dealer, manager of an apartment house, painter, or a doctor. You must learn to assume responsibilities, and be willing to serve others, and give counsel freely. You are efficient and methodical. Negative aspects which you should avoid are being stubborn, domineering, exacting, and unreasonable. You usually want your own way, imposing your ideas and ideals on others. You should live in an artistic surrounding, and promote harmony within your home. You are an idealist at heart, and are capable of doing much good for mankind.

Number 7–Specialization

You should choose a field of specialized work, for you should be a thinker, scientist, perfectionist, and an analyst. You must not accept anything unless it can be proven or can be related to facts. You should have a good mind and be able to accumulate knowledge from all sources. Your appeal is to individuals. You must have time to be alone to study, meditate, and commune with the higher forces of nature. Your work should be professional rather than business or manual labor. You will succeed as an educator, scientist, lawyer, teacher, writer, organist, florist, religious worker, or teacher, specialist, tutor, or in medicine, law, invention, radio, acting or the occult sciences. You can be an inspiration to others.

Number 8—Executive Ability or Finance

You should learn to be an organizer, for you have latent executive ability and could manage large corporations. You must learn to be practical, efficient, and a good judge of character. You were meant to be a leader, either in your own business or for the public. You have a philosophical point of view, yet you are persevering, well-balanced, and just. Your best success will come when you strike a balance between making money and spiritual endeavors, for you may strain so hard to acquire wealth that you may wear yourself out and detract the very thing you are striving to achieve. You could succeed well as a judge, lawyer, banker, financial advisor, engineer, broker, character analyst, surgeon, or in general business, athletic activities, real estate, the publishing business, or in governmental work.

Number 9—Universalist

You must learn to be a humanitarian, for you should love mankind and aim at all times to help others. Your appeal is to the many rather than the few. You must learn to be selfless and impersonal, expecting nothing in return for your efforts. You must learn to be generous, sympathetic, tolerant, and sensitive. You have a good imagination and could succeed as an educator, artist, musician, healer, teacher, writer, reformer, missionary, doctor, social worker, and dealer in health foods or oil. You could also be an entertainer, traveler, or sales manager. You are an idealist, and you often become disappointed when others do not live up to your expectations. You must guard against being moody, timid, and vacillating.

Number 11—Limelight

Since you have a master birthpath much is expected of you. You cannot lead a personal life, for you belong to the public. You are idealistic and inspirational. You would make an excellent lecturer, for the platform was meant for you. You may lean toward religion, and could be a minister or spiritual adviser. You could succeed at anything listed under the number *two*, but your light should shine brighter as you were endowed with many talents. Any field such as a diplomat, lecturer, motion picture director, author, critic, writer, artist, television expert, aviator, advertiser, or electrical worker would be appropriate for you. You may have been born into a family with little spiritual beliefs. As an agnostic you may suffer. You must learn to live humbly in the limelight.

Number 22—Master Builder

You mu.,t learn to be both practical and inspirational. This you can accomplish because you have the idealism of the number *eleven* and the practicality and building qualities of number *four*. You are destined to be a leader, for your capabilities spread over a wide range, even reaching international boundaries. You should command respect, and you can rise to great heights. You would make a good statesman, a great diplomat, a business executive of a large corporation, an organizer, the president or manager of a large enterprise, an ambassador, an analyst, an explorer, an international financier, an athlete, or a promoter. You must learn that justice and service count as well as cooperation. You may be born with a physical handicap such as being a cripple, or with mental limitations.

EIGHT

Your Birthday--What It Tells You About Your Talents

Your birthday, or the specific day of any month of any year, specifies the talents you brought with you into this life—and the tools you have accumulated to make them work for you. While the influence of your birthday is potent all of your life, it is most effective between your twenty-eighth and fifty-sixth birthday, the middle or the most active period or cycle of your life.

WHAT YOUR BIRTHDAY TELLS YOU IN NUMEROLOGY

Birthdays range from the first through the thirty-first day inclusive, for they follow the days within a calendar month. Their meaning is the same regardless of the month or year of birth. Since birthdays are one of the *three cycles* on a birthpath, they cannot be isolated and treated alone in choosing a vocation, for they are the talents or tools to be used in connection with the entire birthpath. The birthday greatly influences the birthpath, and helps you to choose your right vocation.

The meaning of birthdays for every day in the month is set out as follows:

Number One Birthday

If your birthday is on the first day of any month, if you are living constructively, you are independent, original, creative, a pioneer, and a natural leader. You are inclined to procrastinate, for you find excuses for not finishing what you start. You like to tell others how things should be done rather than do them yourself. Having a fine mind, you can reason things out. You should follow several lines, or have an avocation rather than specialize in one endeavor. While you are sensitive and feel deeply, you are undemonstrative, and are often considered "cold," or unresponsive. Even though you seldom show affection, you want sympathy, praise, and encouragement. You are practical as well as idealistic and individualistic. Occupations which bring you before the public are right for you such as being a salesman, air pilot, engineer, inventor, analyst, teacher, advertiser, or writer.

Number Two Birthday

If your birthday is on the second day of any month, you are a peacemaker or arbitrator. You work better in a group or for another than in an individual capacity. Being fond of music and rhythm, you have considerable talent for dancing, playing an instrument, or for writing poetry. You are tactful, diplomatic, and cooperative, but you are very sensitive and emotional. You are well liked by everyone, and should strive to overcome your periodic moods of depression. You are inclined to underestimate your ability. Therefore, you are in danger of becoming a doormat for someone else. You may succeed in civic service or governmental work, or as a politician, analyst, librarian, clerk, detail worker, police officer, or in an artistic pursuit such as painting, music, or dancing. Having a deep love nature you want and need affection.

Number Three Birthday

If your birthday is on the third day of any month, individual self-expression in any of the arts such as speaking, writing, painting, or acting is necessary for your happiness and content-ment. You are intellectual, artistic, and creative. You enjoy being with people and have many friends, for you have an excellent sense of humor and are a good entertainer. You are liked by both sexes, and are an addition to any group, for you have a vivid imagination and you are a good story teller. You should engage in several occupations, for you must keep yourself busy. You must be careful lest you become critical. You have the ability to recover quickly from any illness. You are easily satisfied, and tend to make the best of any situation.

You should do some literary work, as you can make the simplest incident appear exciting or thrilling.

You belong before the public in such occupations as a lecturer, writer, musician, actor, advertiser, lawyer, doctor, beautician, health or food operator, gourmet cook, or hostess. You may be interested in metaphysical subjects.

Number Four Birthday

If your birthday is on the fourth day of any month, you are materially inclined and belong in the business world. You are orderly, sympathetic, economical, and honest. Since you are a practical person, you should lay a good foundation. While you have a love nature, you discipline yourself to the extent that you dislike showing any affection. You are a tireless worker, and are good at detail. You drive yourself and others to finish quickly what you have started. You have a negative tendency to be stubborn and set in your ways. You often lack tact, which is due to bending backwards to be truthful. You dislike change, but you should learn to play some of the time.

You could succeed as a contractor, architect, draftsman, mechanic, clerk, office manager, builder, soldier, auditor, stenographer, efficiency expert, or in civil service or governmental work.

Number Five Birthday

If you birthday is on the fifth day of any month, you are psychically inclined and should follow your hunches. You are intellectual, versatile, investigative, and imaginative. You must learn to handle the opposite sex. You should welcome experiences and change. Radiating enthusiasm, you have a magnetic personality. Therefore, you could be a good salesman. You should marry young to stabilize yourself, but you may be a difficult marriage partner, for you dislike being tied down and disciplined. You should do considerable traveling.

You could succeed in a brokerage business, or a salesman, diagnostician, insurance adjuster, analyst, editor, chemist, vocational director, athletic coach, or in stocks and bonds.

Number Six Birthday

If your birthday is on the sixth day of any month, you are deeply rooted in the home and the community, for you have a deep love nature. You would make a devoted parent, although you would love children even though they were not your own. Praise and appreciation are essential to your happiness, for you need companionship, love, approval, and are miserable if criticized. You must assume responsibilities in the community as well as in your home. You are inclined to be stubborn and argumentative. You are a perfectionist, and are always looking for your ideal which you seldom find.

You should be interested in music, especially in singing or playing a musical instrument. You belong in a field which promotes health, beauty, or comfort. You have a fine sense of mimicry or imitation, for you are mental rather than intellectual.

You should succeed in civic or community work, music, painting, acting, or as the head of an institution such as an orphan's home or a retiree center. Other fields harmonious for you are in the hotel or restaurant business, operating a health center, beauty parlor, a chef, florist, costume designing, or owning a small business.

Number Seven Birthday

If your birthday is on the seventh of any month, you are a perfectionist. You are individualistic and should specialize in some scientific line, as you have a keen reasoning mind and are capable of deep mental analysis. You are very psychic and sensitive, and should follow your hunches. It is best for you to work alone, since you do not take orders well from others. You should avoid gambling and speculating. Never enter into a partnership on a 50-50 basis. Marriage can be unsuccessful, especially if you choose a mate born on the 15th, 24th, or 26th of any month. You are inclined to be self-centered and stubborn.

You could succeed as a scientist, writer, landscape gardener, teacher, occultist, surgeon, banker, dealer in antiques and jewelry, or a broker.

Number Eight Birthday

If your birthday is on the eighth day of any month, you belong in the business world, for you are progressive, creative, and have executive ability. You are a good judge of values. Eight is considered a lucky birthday for making money, for you need never know want if you live constructively. While you have an excellent financial birthday, if your name is out of harmony with your birthday, you may experience difficult circumstances during the latter years of your life. You like to make a good impression, and you should own or be at the head of a business. You would like to own a choice library, but you are more interested in owning than reading books. You are fond of display and large gestures, such as donating money to institutions or becoming a collector.

You could succeed as a banker, lawyer, executive, engineer, personnel director, orchestra leader, accountant, or manufacturer.

Number Nine Birthday

If your birthday is on the ninth day of any month, you are essentially a philanthropist and humanitarian, for you are considered the big brother to all. You are artistic and intellectual. You can be reached through your emotions, which will make you generous. You should avoid marriage in a nine cycle, since nine is a finisher and you may end up in a divorce or some type of separation. You may do considerable traveling and be subject to many changes. You will have many disappointments, and may experience loss or separation of your loved ones.

You could succeed in artistic or literary pursuits such as acting, dramatics, writing, teaching, painting, landscape gardening, interior decorating, or in oil, insurance, advertising, traveling, lecturing, or in religious work. Your greatest reward will come from serving others rather than from leading a personal selfish life.

Number Ten Birthday

If your birthday is on the tenth of any month, you should work alone or be at the head of a business, for you dislike taking advice or orders from others. You are not domestically inclined, and prefer not to be involved in home problems. You are creative and original, and could follow any artistic line, especially as an avocation. You should engage in several lines of endeavor. You are an idealist, and are constantly trying to improve your surroundings. You are apt to be jealous of your friends and associates. You may feel alone, for you may be forced to stand on your own feet and receive little help from others. You have a good mind and are fearless.

You could succeed in an individual capacity such as an inventor, promoter, aviator, teacher, lawyer, advertiser, writer, or salesman.

Number Eleven Birthday

If your birthday is on the eleventh day of any month, you have high ideals and aspirations. You have a master birthday, and are governed by inspiration. You should avoid being a dreamer rather than a doer. Often you will be vacilllating in your desires, and not be practical. Be careful lest your intellect overshadow your intuition, for you are psychic and should act upon first impressions without stopping to reason things out. While you may appear to be calm and collected without, you are actually high strung and nervous within. You are emotional and extreme in your loves, and are apt to try to impose your moral standards on others. Avoid being mercenary and miserly with your money. You belong in the limelight before the public.

You could succeed as a lecturer, dancer, auctioneer, promoter, or in fields dealing with electricity, philosophy, art, national advertising, motion picture work, or as a statistician, accountant, or clerk.

Number Twelve Birthday

If your birthday is on the twelfth day of any month, you have a good reasoning mind and are very capable generally. You can express yourself well and to the point. You could qualify as a speaker or writer. You should cultivate tact and diplomacy, for you are apt to be blunt in speech and create enemies. This could block your success. You are very practical and like action. You are inclined to be nervous, and very impatient. You, like all numbers which reduce to three, must learn not to scatter your energies. You are interested in many lines of endeavor, and should be kept intellectually busy or you may suffer from moods of depression. You are a good parent or teacher, but you are a strict disciplinarian. You would make an excellent trial lawyer, as you are convincing and able to win an argument. You have a leaning toward design such as applied in architecture.

You could succeed well as a lawyer, writer, speaker, designer, head of a hospital, doctor, entertainer, promoter, druggist, or advertiser. Other avenues open for you are dealing in health foods, running a beauty parlor, or conducting a charm school.

Number Thirteen Birthday

If your birthday is on the thirteenth day of any month, you are down-to-earth in your desires. You could make a good business or office manager as you are orderly, practical, and good at details. You are a hard worker, and will drive yourself as well as others. You need a home background to succeed. You have a strong love nature, but you find it difficult to express yourself. You are apt to be dictatorial, and are often considered unreasonable. You would be attracted to the building industry.

You belong in the business world and could succeed in building, accounting, merchandising, designing, mining, geology, architecture, clerical or stenographic work, wood carving, or in business requiring much detail and statistics. You are not the creative type. Other vocations good for you are an electrician, plumber, or a mechanic. Governmental or political work is also right for you.

Number Fourteen Birthday

If your birthday is on the fourteenth day of any month, you are versatile, dual-natured, and like change or anything new. You are inclined to be lucky at gambling, and like to take a chance. You should marry early in life, for this will act as a stabilizing influence. Be careful lest you fall a victim to bodily vices such as drink, sex, and gambling. You are sympathetic, emotional, and can easily be reached through your feelings. You are psychic, and have a prophetic mind, but you have both constructive and destructive tendencies. You should engage in business rather than in an artistic line.

You could succeed in following your hunches, or in the field of selling, especially travel tours, land-promotional schemes, mining, or in the brokerage business. Another field for you is that of a specialist of eyes, ears, nose, and throat.

Number Fifteen Birthday

If your birthday is on the fifteenth day of any month, you love home life and your family. You would make an excellent teacher or parent, as you are capable and responsible. You should succeed financially, as you have the gift of attracting opportunities and harmonious conditions. You acquire knowledge through observa--

tion, rather than by studying or through research. You will always be youthful and active. Women of this birthday are usually good cooks, but they do not follow recipes.

You are artistically inclined, and are often attracted to music, either playing an instrument or singing. You may succeed in civil service, or in any community work. You are generous and demonstrative, and are capable of much self-sacrifice, often carrying the burden of older people. You may be argumentative and rather stubborn.

You may succeed in intellectual or artistic pursuits such as teaching, nursing, lecturing, medicine, singing, costume designing, or the publishing business. Institutional, hospital, community, or civic endeavors are other fields in which you could be successful.

Number Sixteen Birthday

If your birthday is on the sixteenth day of any month, you are a perfectionist. You often become moody and brood when others fail to live up to your standards. You are inclined to be a lone wolf and aloof, but you actually want affection. You should engage in some business which will give you wide worldly contacts. Country living or in the suburbs is a good place to calm your nerves. You are very psychic and should follow your hunches. This is often difficult, because you are naturally analytical and try to reason things out. Your dreams are often prophetic in meaning. You do not like to have anyone interefere with your plans, even though you are retiring, and you often procrastinate.

You could succeed in scientific work which requires specialization such as an educator, writer, editor, lawyer, florist, metallurgist, or in landscape gardening. The color of purple will protect you from adverse conditions.

Number Seventeen Birthday

If your birthday is on the seventeenth day of any month, you have a fortunate birthday, good for business. You may be very shrewd and ruthless in business, although you are essentially honest. You are set in your ways, and seldom can be swayed from your idea. You are like a seesaw, conservative and high-minded one minute, and extravagant the next. You would make an excellent banker, for you work well in an executive position with subordinates working under you doing the detail or routine work. You are materially inclined, not spiritually, as you demand proof. You should be the head of your own business, or deal in expansion over a wide field. You may be drawn toward writing, but it will be in the technical or historical field.

You will succeed as an actuary, editor, publisher, banker, broker, librarian, lawyer, executive, or in business connected with the earth, such as in oil, mining, or stocks.

Number Eighteen Birthday

If your birthday is on the eighteenth day of any month, you may have many disappointments, losses, and changes until you learn to live for others and not for your own personal aggrandizement. You would make an excellent surgeon, for great things are expected of you. You have an active birthday subject to change and travel. You may be required to bear the burden of the sick, helpless, and aged. You are intellectual, emotional, and refined, but you like to argue, and are often critical of others. You are capable of being very independent and efficient, and have the ability to give advice wisely. You love music and art, and could be a dramatic critic or writer.

You could succeed as a surgeon, lawyer, actor, artist, or in business dealing in railroads, oil, stocks, journeys, politics, religion, or statistics.

Number Nineteen Birthday

If your birthday is on the nineteenth day of any month, you are independent, artistic, and original. You are subject to extremes, either rising to the clouds or falling into a pit. You like change and versatility, and always want to better conditions. Since the number nineteen vibration includes all numbers from one to nine inclusive, the effects are far reaching. You belong in the professional rather than the business field. You are nervous and succumb to anger easily, but you do not hold a grudge and soon forget the incident. You seldom find complete happiness in marriage, for you may feel you are alone even though you are married. You do not like to follow conventions. You may have to make many adjustments, since you refuse to take advice from others and must learn through bitter experience.

You will succeed well as a forceful politician, musician,

designer, lawyer, inventor, salesman, electrician, aviator, automotive worker, or as a medical specialist.

Number Twenty Birthday

If your birthday is on the twentieth day of any month, you are a natural peacemaker. You could be an excellent politician, or do well in governmental work. You should own your own small business or work for a small concern, as you have a tendency to be satisfied to work with and for others rather than direct them in large enterprises. You are musical, love beauty, and could sing. You are diplomatic and tactful, and fond of your family. Because of your strong love nature, you should be careful to stick up for your own rights, as people are prone to take advantage of you, or treat you as a doormat.

You could succeed as a politician, statistician, musician, clerk, accountant, stenographer, office worker, librarian, author, collector, singer, or as an analyst.

Number Twenty-one Birthday

If your birthday is on the twenty-first day of any month, you are socially inclined. You ary interested in so many things that you must be careful, or you will scatter your endeavors too much. You must learn to concentrate, as you find it difficult to finish what you start. You are also nervous and somewhat erratic. You might be drawn to dramatics, as you can effectively entertain others. You make a better friend than a partner in marriage, for you may be suspicious and impatient. You are emotional and subject to the up-and-down moods of all threes, but you should cultivate being cheerful and not moody.

You may succeed in any line of expression in which you use words, such as writing, speaking, or acting, for you are a good mimic. Other fields for you are advertising, law, medicine, publishing, dancing, journalism, as well as fields of music and art.

Number Twenty-two Birthday

If your birthday is on the twenty-second day of any month you have a master birthday. You can function well in the material or business world. You must be careful to keep an equal balance between your emotions and the practical side of your nature. You are nervous and highstrung, and need much rest. You should be a universalist and not interested solely in personal achievement, for your power is far-reaching. You have hunches which you should follow, for you are very intuitive. Since everything happens doubly to you, you should make an effort to live constructively and harmoniously. You have such a deep nature, that at times you do not understand yourself. You should develop tact and organization ability, doing woık before the public in large groups.

You could succeed well as an ambassador, real estate promoter, corporation lawyer, organizer of chain stores, exporter, buyer, efficiency expert, teacher, mechanic, clerk, engineer, inventor, poet, or an evangelist. You must contribute to the general good of mankind.

Number Twenty-three Birthday

If your birthday is on the twenty-third day of any month, you should follow professional pursuits instead of the business line. You would make an excellent diagnostician, psychiatrist, or healer. You belong in the intellectual world as you are a quick thinker. You may be interested in chemistry, physical culture, salesmanship, or in the brokerage business. You have a charming personality, and can deal well with the opposite sex, in fact, better than with your own sex. Your aim should be high, for it is necessary for you to be proud of your accomplishments. You are socially inclined.

You may succeed as a teacher of physical culture, diagnostician, nurse, psychiatrist, psychologist, writer, scientist, actor, broker, entertainer, traveler, sculptor, salesman, or as a golf expert.

Number Twenty-four Birthday

If your birthday is on the twenty-fourth day of any month, you are a natural mother or teacher, for your love is concentrated on your family and loved ones. You may be asked to care for elderly people. You would make an excellent nurse or doctor. You are a natural cook. Your interest also should be in the community doing civic work. You may be inclined to be stubborn and argumentative, but you are a solid citizen. You have a pleasant speaking voice, and you could specialize in singing. Since you have a personality that attracts, you should go after what you want personally and not resort to writing letters or to telephoning. You should watch for the negative tendencies of jealousy, laziness, fault-finding, and worry.

You may succeed as a teacher, nurse, civic worker, cook, restuaranteur, musician, doctor, merchant, minister, or as the head of a civic institution.

Number Twenty-five Birthday

If your birthday is on the twenty-fifth day of any month, you are a perfectionist setting as high a standard for yourself as for others. You are intuitive and prophetic, and should be interested in metaphysical subjects. You must learn to concentrate in order to be forceful and stable, for you often fluctuate. You should live close to nature in the country or suburbs, for the quietude will calm your nerves. Your greatest fault lies in underestimating your own ability. Your first reaction to any proposition is usually "no." Therefore, you should think and weigh matters deeply before you make a decision. Avoid being lazy, critical, and erratic.

You may succeed as a naturopath specialist, scientist, politician, statistician, painter, student of the occult, F.B.I. investigator, lawyer, teacher, writer, or as a detective, since nothing remains hidden from you.

Number Twenty-six Birthday

If your birthday is on the twenty-sixth day of any month, you should enter the business field, for you are good at figures, an excellent organizer, and a good business executive. You should be careful to finish what you start. This is a good financial birthday. You need never know the pinch of want, for you have the power to attract money, people, or whatever is necessary, even late in life. You must cultivate optimism, and refrain from living in the past. You are particular about your family, your belongings, and you are fond of show, for you like to make an impression. Since you are subject to extreme emotions, either up-or-down, you should marry early as a stabilizing influence.

You may succeed as an engineer, diplomat, artist, politician, publisher, corporation lawyer, accountant, orchestra leader, actuary, or as a conductor of travel tours.

Number Twenty-seven Birthday

If your birthday is on the twenty-seventh day of any month, you would do well in literary, dramatic, or religious work. You are a natural leader, being forceful, quietly determined, and versatile. You lean toward esoteric teachings, for you are very psychic and mediumistic. Therefore, you should watch that you do not become too involved, for you could easily be disturbed and succumb to its influences. You do not like to account for your conduct. Consequently, you work best in an individual capacity. Like all nines (2 + 7) you cannot lead a purely personal live. Marriage also in a nine cycle could be disappointing. You are very affectionate and emotional, and are somewhat nervous and erratic.

You may succeed in artistic or literary pursuits such as a writer, advertiser, lawyer, doctor, diplomat, journalist, poet, teacher, broker, healer, stock-dealer, artist, realtor, actor, landscape gardener, insurance salesman, lecturer, or as a salesman of food, health, or beauty products.

Number Twenty-eight Birthday

If your birthday is on the twenty-eighth day of any month, you are very affectionate and have high ideals. You are independent, strong-willed, and are willing to sacrifice much to achieve your goal. You love freedom, but often you suffer from limitations. You like to begin things, but often you fail to finish them. You may be a daydreamer, which may lead to laziness if you do not curb this tendency. Be careful not to lose interest the minute you achieve success. You are inclined to magnify your troubles, and so you are subject to many disappointments.

You could succeed as a teacher, electrician, inventor, aviator, lawyer, salesman, decorator, advertiser, engineer, fashion director, or as a scientist. You are an executive by nature.

Number Twenty-nine Birthday

If your birthday is on the twenty-ninth of any month, you have a very strong birthday. Two plus nine adds up to eleven, which is a master number. This can be a prosperous birthday if properly directed. You are an extremist, either joyful or depressed. You must learn to straighten out your path and help others to adjust theirs. You are often so absorbed in dreams, ideals, and worries that you fail to give consideration to others. You should seek a definite interest to keep you calm and well-balanced. You may turn to religion, for you can be inspirational. You prefer many casual friends to a few intimate ones. Your name should be in harmony with your birthpath to succeed. You need a home background, but you are not always easy to live with.

You may succeed in aviation, electrical or automotive work, selling, law, teaching, radio, speaking, or dealing in food commodities.

Number Thirty Birthday

If your birthday is on the thirtieth day of any month, individual self-expression is necessary for your happiness, just as it is for all birthdays which reduce to *three*. You could be a good manager, but you do not like hard work. You are fond of dramatics, and could act, or be a mimic. You are set in your opinions, and always think you are right. You have a good imagination and possess some intuitive qualities, but you should guard against all obsessions, and not take excursions into the mystical realm.

You may succeed as an advertiser, teacher, social worker, writer, artist, speaker, manager, or in the health, beauty, or food line. Any field which requires the use of words would be harmonious for you.

Number Thirty-one Birthday

If your birthday is on the thirty-first day of any month, you are a practical builder, and have good business ability. You are a very hard worker, honest, loyal, determined, and thrifty. You neither forget a kindness nor an injury. You should never delve in psychic phenomena. You should marry early, as you need responsibility for stabilization purposes. You love travel, and do not like to live alone. You are inclined to be stubborn and set in your ways. You set very high standards for yourself, and may be disappointed when you fail to reach your expectations.

You could succeed as a pharmacist or chemist, as you have a natural knowledge of drugs. Other fields for you are an accountant, clerk, architect, office manager, efficiency expert, stenographer, contractor, statistician, or a draftsman. You could also do well in the manufacturing business, or in the military service as a leader.

HOW TO USE THE POWER OF CONCORDS
IN NUMEROLOGY

All birthdays are grouped into three classes called *concords.* They are the air (artistic), water (scientific), and the fire (business) concords.

AIR OR ARTISTIC CONCORD

Birthdays which reduce to *three, six,* or *nine* are in the *air or artistic concord. Three* is the cornerstone, *six* the key, and *nine* the capstone, forming a triangle. The element of air is spirit.

Individuals with birthdays in this concord want to have freedom in thought and movement. They are artistic, literary, expressive, and impersonal people. They are often very talkative, even chatterboxes at times, intangible, and very active. They belong before the public either in speaking, writing, or acting, for they constitute the inspirational type.

The air birthdays of any month are the *third, sixth, ninth, twelfth, fifteenth, eighteenth, twenty-first, twenty-fourth, twenty-seventh,* and the *thirtieth.* This concord produces writers, artists, actors, doctors, lawyers, musicians, and advertisers.

Examples of Birthdays in the Artistic Concord:

February 3rd	June 12th
March 6th	July 18th
May 9th	August 24th

WATER OR SCIENTIFIC CONCORD

Birthdays which reduce to *one, five,* or *seven* are in the *water or scientific concord. One* is the cornerstone, *five,* the key, and *seven* the capstone. The element of water is mind. Therefore, those who have birthdays in this concord should study and accumulate much knowledge. Number *one* people are creative, original, intellectual, and scientific. Number *five* indivuduals are changeable, restless, magnetic in personality, and versatile. They can be erratic. Number *seven* people are studious, often psychic, retiring, analytical, and scientific. All three are intuitive.

The *water birthdays* of any month are the *first, fifth, seventh, tenth, fourteenth, sixteenth, twenty-third, twenty-fifth,* and the *twenty-eighth.* They should choose engineering, aviation, salesmanship, writing, teaching, managing an individual business, or being a diagnostician or scientist.

Examples of Birthdays in the Scientific Concord Are:

February 1st	June 19th
April 5th	August 23rd
May 7th	December 25th

FIRE OR BUSINESS CONCORD

Birthdays which reduce to *two, four, eight, eleven,* and twenty-two are in the *fire or business concord.* The *eleven* and the *twenty-two* are master numbers. Individuals with birthdays in this concord will gravitate to the business world. They are enthusiastic, aggressive, and have masculine qualities. The element of fire is feeling. Consequently they are called the emotional type. Actually, they are considered austere or cold individuals, for they find it difficult to express their feelings.

The *fire birthdays* of any month are the *second, fourth, eighth, eleventh, thirteenth, seventeenth, twentieth, twenty-second, twenty-sixth, twenty-ninth,* and the *thirty-first.* They make successful business managers, bankers, contractors, merchants, auditors, stenographers, business executives, designers, and politicians.

Examples of Birthdays in the Business Concord:

January 2nd	October 11th
March 4th	November 22nd
June 8th	December 29th

NINE

Your Final Opportunity or Goal Power Number

Your *power number* is your beacon light directing you throughout your life span, but it is most noticeable and effective during the latter part of your life. It acts as a summation of all of your personal numbers, putting them under one focus or final goal.

HOW TO FIND YOUR POWER NUMBER

You can find your power number by adding together your total birthpath and your total destiny number. This means adding together the total letters of your original name at birth (destiny) and reducing this to a final number, and your total birthpath, which includes the day, month, and year of your birth, and reducing this to a single digit. It is a very simple method to follow. Your power number is your signpost guiding you to latter days of enjoyment, relaxation, and even profit. We'll now set up a few samples for you to follow.

Lawrence Welk, who is well known for his famous orchestra, was born on March 11, 1903.

L A W R E N C E W E L K   March 11, 1903 = (11 + 7)

3 1 5 9 5 5 3 5   5 5 3 2   3 11 13   9
      36   15   4
      9   +   6 = 15 = 6 (6 + 9 = 15 = 6) (power number.)

The total of his destiny number is six. His birthpath totals

(11 + 7) with an underlying nine. His destiny (6) plus his birthpath (9) total six, which is his *power number.*

Lawrence Welk's power number is six, which is very potent because it combines the two most important numbers in a numeroscope, namely, the destiny and birthpath numbers.

Now before you figure your own, we'll set up another example.

$$A N N A \quad E L E A N O R \quad R O O S E V E L T$$

$$\underline{1\ 5\ 5\ 1} \quad \underline{5\ 3\ 5\ 1\ 5\ 6\ 9} \quad \underline{9\ 6\ 6\ 1\ 5\ 4\ 5\ 3\ 2}$$

$$\frac{12}{3} \qquad \frac{34}{7} \qquad \frac{41}{5} = 15 = 6$$

$$\underline{\text{October 11 1884}}$$

$$\underline{10 \quad 11 \quad 21}$$

$$1\ +\ 11\ +\ 3 = (11 - 4) = 6$$

Power number is Destiny (6) plus Birthpath (6) = 3.

$$(6 + 6 = 12 = 1 + 2 = 3)$$

You will also notice that her full name was in perfect harmony with her birthpath, making success imminent. Her power number of three gave her free self-expression. She was an excellent speaker and journalist.

Now set up your name and date of birth and reduce these to a single total. Follow the four steps given below.

Summary:

Step 1. To find your power number set up your full given name and reduce this to a single digit.

Step 2. Add your full date of birth and reduce this to a single digit.

Step 3. Add together the totals of your name and birth numbers.

Step 4: Consult the table page 97 and read what is in store for you now and in your later years.

Notice: For further details refer to the corresponding number under "General Meaning of Numbers" in Chapter Two.

MEANING OF POWER NUMBERS

Number One

You will be given the opportunity for leadership. You will be very independent, creative, original, and active. You can be a pioneer in a new field. You will be ambitious, clever, and aggressive. You must avoid being too opinionated, domineering, and set in your ways. For further information see attributes of Number 1 under "General Meaning of Numbers" in Chapter Two.

Number Two

Now is the time to participate in one of the fine arts, such as music, art, and dancing. Since you have the qualities of a diplomat, you can get along with others and get them to cooperate. Counseling, or any advisory capacity would prove successful and enjoyable for you. You like collecting and gathering data, and you may lean toward an interest in libraries and museums. Being spiritually inclined, you may turn to religion. You must avoid being a doormat. (See Number 2 under "General Meaning of Numbers" in Chapter Two.)

Number Three

This is your opportunity for true self-expression in words, either in speaking, writing, or acting. Give speeches on the subject of your choice, or entertain on the platform for you have a talent for the use of words, and a good sense of humor. You are creative, and have a good imagination. Don't waste time now scattering your talents, but work toward a definite goal. (See Number 3 under "General Meaning of Numbers" in Chapter Two.)

Number Four

If you have built a practical foundation, you can now realize your goal and put your ideas to work, but it will require considerable effort. Your tenacity of purpose, plus the fact that you are sympathetic, orderly, and honest, will help you strengthen your foundation for success. You may turn to scientific or religious pursuits, but they will be of the orthodox nature, and not that of a new approach. You will be forced to stick your nose to the grindstone, but the outcome will be rewarding. (See Number 4 Characteristics under "General Meaning of Numbers" for further details in Chapter Two.)

Number Five

This is your chance for much experience. You will be free to travel extensively, and be very active in a new project, for you have an inquisitive mind. However, your activities should be geared toward the improvement and advancement of the general public. This is no time to rest. Be sure to sift your interests. Five is symbolical of the five-pointed star, but it is often too diversified, for it may reach out in too many directions at this period of life. You should be selective, and concentrate on one major accomplishment. (See Number 5 Characteristics under "General Meaning of Numbers" for further details in Chapter Two.)

Number Six

Your opportunity for service is at its zenith. This applies more to community work than just for your own immediate family, for the six power number is impersonal. You can have the comforts of home, for you are well protected and loved, and you have financial satisfaction. You will still need to assume responsibility, for you are the cosmic parent. All tools for success are present. (See Number 6 under "General Meaning of Numbers" for further details in Chapter Two.)

Number Seven

You now have the opportunity to follow mental and spiritual pursuits. As an educator, others will seek you out for your knowledge and wisdom. You may wish to be alone to retire and meditate. You may even write on metaphysical subjects or follow some unusual inventive or scientific line of endeavor. You may become an introvert. (See Number 7 of "General Meaning of Numbers" for further details in Chapter Two.)

Number Eight

You now have the chance for expansion, fame, power, and recognition. You will need to discipline yourself, for executive ability will be required. This is your chance for analysis, research, and counseling. Supervising and directing the affairs of others can be your goal. You may be drawn to real estate. (See Number 8 Characteristics of "General Meaning of Numbers" for further details in Chapter Two.)

Number Nine

Now you can be a big brother to all of humanity. You must have a universal outlook, for the world is your battlefield. You should strive for an impersonal life, for personal interests may be disappointing. The fields of drama, literature, and the arts are open to you. Philanthropy and service can be rewarding. (See Number 9 Characteristics of "General Meaning of Numbers" for further details in Chapter Two.)

Number Eleven

You will now have the opportunity to appear in the limelight, for you could be a leader. You may be drawn to the platform. Many idealists such as religious leaders and evangelists have this power number, for it can be inspirational and spiritual in effect. You may want to be a crusader for peace, or for any good cause. The field of aviation, electricity, television, or invention may also appeal to you. Fame and distinction may be your reward if you have prepared yourself previously. (See also Number Two under General Meaning of Numbers in Chapter Two for additional details.)

Number Twenty-two

This is your chance for both national and international recognition if you have built a good foundation. You should be both a practical builder and an idealist. Many great statesmen, as well as ambassadors, have this power number, for it has universal rather than personal appeal. You must work for the benefit of the world as well as for yourself. (See also Number Four characteristics under General Meaning of Numbers in Chapter Two.)

When I first began to study Numerology, I became very discouraged because I believed I was not the person indicated by my numbers, and that my chart failed to give a true picture of myself. The reason is that when I listed or enumerated the numbers under my full given name at birth, the chart indicated that I had a missing digit of number one, which stands for lack of originality, independence, and aggressiveness. I felt confident that I had considerable initiative and creative ideas, and that I certainly was not a doormat or shrinking violet. I realized later, that I had failed to take into consideration my power number. The total of my destiny number (7) and birthpath (3) equals 10 (power number), which not only accounts for the one, but it is ten times stronger than a one and suggests the potential of super-independence and originality.

HOW YOU CAN PREPARE FOR A HAPPY OLD AGE

Your life was mapped out for you at your birth, but most of you have been too busy earning a living and assuming the responsibilities of a family, to be cognizant of the powers and force behind the power number until you have time to reevaluate your life. The latter years can be the best in your entire life span, for then the power number can be operating full force. It indicates one more experience or lesson to be learned, and one more opportunity. One way to prepare for this is to have a hobby or avocation, which you can pursue at full speed later.

TEN

How to Know Your Challenges: Warning Signs as to Your Stumbling Blocks

WHERE TO FIND YOUR CHALLENGES

A challenge is found on a person's birthpath. By establishing the downward triangle or pyramid, using the month, day and year of birth, you can, by studying the final numerological factor, learn what your deficiencies are and then proceed to surmount the hurdles, thus making the challenge work for you by attracting opportunities, power, and desirable friendships. The final numerological key of the challenge represents the defect, but you must also recognize the numbers behind the final digit as hidden subchallenges, and you must heed their warnings during the periods specified.

HOW YOU CAN OVERCOME YOUR WEAK TRAITS

Life would be mighty dull without its hindrances or challenges to shake you out of your natural lethargy, and force you to fight the elements and drawbacks which prevent you from reaching your goal. A challenge is really a weak trait in your character, or one which may be an undeveloped talent rather than an asset which is entirely lacking. It represents a trait of character which must be strengthened through your willpower, if you expect to overcome its difficulties. It acts as a stumbling block or a warning sign, urging you to "beware" of its pitfalls, for it need not dominate you.

Your challenge is not the same as anyone else's, for it varies with each individual. However, some challenges appear more often than others. They are the *one, two,* and *three. Four* and *five* are next in frequency. *Six* and *seven* seldom appear as challenges. Eight is never found except in connection with the 0. Nine is never found as a challenge, for it is a universal number.

RULES FOR FINDING YOUR CHALLENGE.

Your challenge is indicated in your birthpath and you will use the rule of subtraction. If a master number appears in your birthdate, you should reduce this to a single digit before subtracting. Now let us proceed as follows:

Step 1: Subtract the digit of the month and the digit of the day from each other. This is your *first* subchallenge.

Step 2: Subtract the digit of the day and the digit of the year from each other. This is your *second subchallenge.*

Step 3: Subtract the two remaining numbers from each other. This is your *third and most important challenge.*

Step 4: Subtract the digit of the month and the digit of the year. This is your *fourth challenge,* which is subordinate to your *third* or main one. Usually the third and fourth challenges will be the same. If they vary, then you have more than one challenge. It means that during the latter part of your life, another challenge is added to the one operating throughout most of your life. This will require understanding, and an additional effort to sustain order, organization, and a balance in your life.

To give you some practice let's set up a hypothetical birthday to figure the challenge. See Figure 10-1.

To find the first subchallenge you subtract the month (December = 12 = 3) and the digit of the day (8) from each other, namely (8-3 = 5).

To find the second subchallenge, subtract the digit of the day (8) and the digit of the year (1931 = 14 = 5) from each other, thus (8-5 = 3).

To find the third and main challenge subtract the remaining numbers from each other (5-3 = 2).

Example:

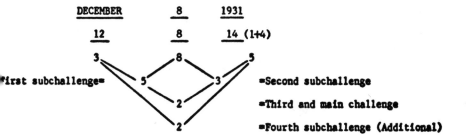

Figure 10-1

To find the fourth and additional challenge subtract the digit of the month (3) and the digit of the year (5) from each other (5-3 = 2).

Number *two* will be the outstanding challenge throughout the life of the individual with the birthpath stated above. The third and fourth challenges are usually the same as stated previously, but we must figure the fourth in case there is an additional challenge. In the case of the above, when the *two* challenge is developed it will be a talent or asset.

Now let's set up another date of birth with a double challenge. See Figure 10-2.

Example:

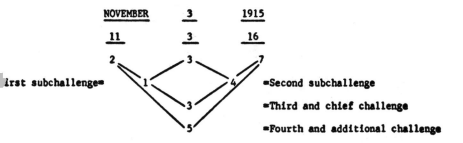

Figure 10-2

This person has a mixed challenge, the three operating all of his life, and the five being added during the latter period of his life. Now let's set up a birthday with a 0 challenge. See Figure 10-3.

Example:

Edward Kennedy was born on February 22, 1932.

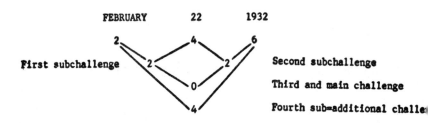

Figure 10-3

The 0 or main challenge indicates that Senator Kennedy. will either have to face and overcome all obstacles, or he will have no obstacle to prevent him from succeeding. In other words, he will either have smooth sailing or constant hindrances to his success. He has the ability to overcome all problems, for he is an old soul, (0), if he will take the effort to do so. He has a choice to make, for he will have many tests. He also has an additional challenge to face in the latter part of his life and that is the *four*. This is difficult, in that he must learn to develop the practical side of his life, and to discipline himself to be punctual, systematic, and orderly. He is apt to dislike work and thriftiness, and must watch lest he become lazy, careless, and stubborn. Hard work is required of him if he expects to overcome this challenge.

Now set up your birthpath (day, month, and year) in a downward triangle as illustrated in this chapter previously and figure your challenge. Follow the four steps given. Then read the meaning of your final challenge according to factors set out later in this chapter. See if you can write a description of what is expected of you depending on your third or main challenge.

While I was shopping with a friend, I noticed she had considerable difficulty deciding on even the most trivial item. She deliberated pro and con as to whether she should purchase an insignificant article. After making her final selection, she again hesitated, fingering the article. In the end, she decided to think the matter over, and so bought nothing.

While driving home together, I asked her if she would mind telling me her date of birth. She said it was November 3, 1915. As I had suspected, her challenge number was *three* (also *five* in the latter part of her life). The *three* indicated indecision.

To cure herself of this indecision, she should force herself to make a quick selection and then stick to her original choice regardless of how much she still wanted to change her mind or vacillate. Eventually through persistence she could overcome the challenge and be able to make a snap judgment, or at least stick to, and be satisfied with, her choice.

MEANING OF THE CHALLENGES
SET OUT IN THIS CHAPTER BY NUMBERS

0

If you have a final challenge or test number of 0, it means one of two things: (1) You must face all challenges, or (2) You have none. You have a choice in your decision, and are expected to choose wisely, as you have the knowledge and talents within you of all the numbers. Or, everything will be an obstacle to hinder your path of progress, and you will have constant struggles or obstacles to overcome, since no definite weakness is indicated for you to strengthen. An old soul is indicated.

1

You must learn to develop a strong willpower, strength of character, and courage, or you will be subjected to being bossed and held down by others, especially your relatives. You will meet with many interferences, but you should not blame others, be resentful, or belligerent. You may find yourself vacillating and turning in every direction to please others, but you will accomplish nothing, not even pleasing yourself, until you become determined to learn to command the respect of others. You have creative and original ideas, but you must put them to use. First ascertain if you are right, and then forge ahead, not with a chip on your shoulder, but firmly.

2

You must develop confidence in yourself or you will become too self-conscious. You are very sensitive and easily hurt. You will find it hard to forgive and forget. Be careful lest you develop an inferiority complex and become a doormat for others. You should stop being hurt at the slightest provocation. You must cultivate a broader viewpoint, and stop referring everything to yourself. Don't copy others, but use your own talents. You like peace, but don't be insincere or avoid the truth just because you want harmony, or be nice just to make an impression. You have considerable psychic power, but you should use it only for personal satisfaction and not for financial gain.

3

You must avoid scattering your talents, for you have a tendency to do too many things at once. You have a fine imagination and a gift for words, but you often find it hard to express yourself effectively. You dislike criticism, and often become a recluse when you should mingle in society and cultivate friends. You should write or lecture, for you are creative. Take an interest in dancing, singing, acting, or speaking so that you are a welcome addition to a group. You must learn not to be extravagant, or to waste time, money, or words. You should not gossip or succumb to moodiness. Instead of burying your talents, you should bring them out so that they will multiply and bring joy to others.

4

If you have a *four* challenge you should discipline yourself to be orderly, punctual, and systematic, for you have a good sense of values which are undeveloped. You are inclined to be lazy, careless, stubborn, and opinionated, as well as being negligent about details and appointments. You dislike work and thriftiness, and are often a procrastinator. Also, you are prone to worry needlessly. You can succeed if you will develop the practical side of your nature. Constant change or restlessness will not be an incentive to doing the hard work that is still required of you.

5

If you have a *five* challenge you want freedom at any price. However, a rolling stone seldom builds a solid foundation. You are curious about sex and the senses. This is a difficult challenge to handle, for it may make you too impulsive. You may want to try everything at least once, and thus cause you to lack stability. Another essential freedom of the five challenge is to learn to let go of people and things. You must cultivate the healthy type of change. You must discern when and what to discard, for that brings progress. Be careful lest you merely want change to satisfy your carnal desires. Desire for freedom may also be due to wanting to escape from responsibilities. A number five challenge is excellent at dealing with the public in work such as promotion, advertising, travel, or publicity. You should learn to control your impulses.

6

If you have a *six* challenge, you are idealistic, but you may also be domineering and meddlesome. You may want everyone to conform to your principles or way of thinking. You may be too positive about what you consider right and wrong. You will quarrel with anyone who disagrees with the rules you have made. This often causes a rift with your marriage partner, as you believe everyone makes mistakes but yourself. You would succeed better if you harnessed yourself to your ideals and tried to make them materialize, rather than cling to people and try to remake them. You will never be completely happy, or find love or appreciation, until you learn that others have a right to their own ideas and standards.

7

If you have a *seven* challenge you will find yourself rebellious against prevailing conditions, but unfortunately you will make no effort to alter or better them, or work for the promotion of something new. This is a tragic and difficult challenge to bear, but luckily very few people have the seven challenge to face. It usually brings a big test or repression. Too much false pride, aloofness, and reserve, keep the real feelings hidden below the surface. You need a good education, so that you can develop keen analysis and technical skills. You should avoid fits of melancholia, and refrain from resorting to drinking. You have an underlying spiritual quality, but you devote too much time to dwelling on your limitations. Consequently, you attract fear instead of faith. If you study and perfect your skills, you can attract the best in life.

8

If you have an *eight* challenge, you have an excellent chance for recognition and promotion if your motives are above reproach. Usually you strain after money and power. Personal freedom based on material possessions is your chief aim. You have a false sense of values, for you fear lack, loss, or limitations and so invite this condition. You must learn that money belongs to everyone and not just to yourself. The *eight* challenge usually appears with a cipher, which governs either the first thirty-five years or the latter part of your life. If 0 appears as a first sub-challenge, it indicates you can be a self-made man. The *eight* challenge causes much strain. You should develop a philosophical frame of mind in order to see both sides of a situation. You can succeed by standing squarely on your own feet, and seeking a balance of realities.

9

Number *nine* does not appear as a challenge. Nine being the highest single digit, it cannot be subtracted from and still have nine as a remainder.

Every human being has a weak line or challenge in his makeup. No task is too difficult for you to handle, for you have the ability to accomplish all that is required of you in this lifetime. Meeting a challenge head-on, and resolving to cross its hurdles by using talents constructively, builds character. Then you will encounter a decided change in your life toward progress and success. This is one of the great rewards of knowing your challenges through numerology.

ELEVEN

Your Pinnacles: How to Know What You Will Face or Experience

Your pinnacles are comparable to an examination or a test which you must face and take, for you cannot escape or avoid their experiences. Their predictions are accurate, whether or not you are equipped to meet their demands.

WHERE YOU CAN FIND YOUR PINNACLES

Pinnacles are found on the birthpath. By setting up an upward triangle or pyramid, using the month, day, and year of your birth as your basis, the four peaks or pinnacles show definite changes in your life. Remember, challenges point downward to form a triangle on your birthpath, while pinnacles point upward.

HOW TO LET YOUR PINNACLE GUIDE YOU

All of you have reached a crossroad or fork in the road of your life where a decision had to be made for following the right road. At that time it would have been profitable to consult your pinnacle number to see under what influence you were then operating, and what future pinnacle you faced. Your pinnacle, or signpost, will point to the direction in which you should travel for best results. It will not only suggest your opportunities, but also the obstacles which, while seemingly castastrophic at the time, were actually "blessings in disguise." Studying your pinnacles will help you understand changes in your moods, your attitudes toward people and things, and your general ups and downs. None of these conditions are disastrous if you understand and are ready to accept them, for they serve as a protective measure for you.

To illustrate the foregoing, if a *seven* pinnacle appears as a period on your birthpath, you may experience much loneliness unless you have devoted at least part of your previous years to learning to live alone. without being lonely, and to develop the studious side of your nature. Social and material affairs will be at a low ebb and very disappointing while transiting this pinnacle. A *nine* pinnacle is often disappointing because of the difficulties and losses involved. It can and will be rewarding when you understand its requirements and have learned to live an impersonal and universal life.

DURATION OF PINNACLES

The cycle of *nine* operates in determining the length of a pinnacle. A circle contains 360 degrees and can be divided into four ninety degree sections $(3 + 6 + 0 = 9)$. Using nine as the cycle of man and four as the periods of attainment, we arrive at 4 x 9 = 36, our basic starting point for figuring the pinnacles. In order to find the duration of the first pinnacle, you subtract the number of the birthpath from thirty-six. To arrive at the length of the second pinnacle, we add nine years to the end of the first pinnacle. For the third period, we add another nine years at the end of the second pinnacle. The fourth pinnacle begins at the end of the third period and is effective until the end of life. The basis for figuring the pinnacle numbers is the birthpath. The following rules should be observed:

RULES FOR FINDING YOUR PINNACLES

FIRST PINNACLE: Add the digit of the month to the digit of the day.
SECOND PINNACLE: Add the digit of the day to the digit of the year.
THIRD PINNACLE: Add together the first and second pinnacles.
FOURTH PINNACLE: Add together the digits of the month and year of birth.

To illustrate the foregoing, we will set up the birthpath of Helen Hayes Brown, born on October 10, 1900. The first lady of the theatre is known by the name of Helen Hayes, and her birthpath can be set up as an example. See Figure 11-1

Subtracting the birthpath, which is three, from thirty-six we learn that the extent of the first pinnacle of two is from birth until she was thirty-three years of age. The second pinnacle of two continues for nine years from her thirty-fourth year until she was forty-three years of age. The third pinnacle of four, which also has a duration of nine years, terminates in her fifty-second year. The fourth pinnacle of two began at age fifty-three and will extend until the end of her life. It is unusual to have so many identical pinnacles of two, but you will notice that all of the cycles on her birthpath are ten (October = 10), (Day = 10), and (1900 = 10). No matter where the one occurs, it always signifies independence and leadership, while the two suggests artistic talents, especially an excellent voice either in speaking or singing.

Since this is slightly complicated, I'll set up another name before you figure your own. See Figure 11-2.

Subtracting the birthpath, which is eleven, from thirty-six we learn that the extent of the first pinnacle of three is from birth until he was twenty-five years of age. The second pinnacle of nine continued for nine years from twenty-six to thirty-five. The third pinnacle of three continued from thirty-six to forty-five. The fourth pinnacle of ten begins at age forty-six and runs until the end of his life. Notice that he is now changing pinnacles, (in 1971), for he is forty-five years of age. He will change his life to something demanding more individualism (10) than pure acting (3).

Now you should be able to set up your own date of birth and figure both the pinnacle and the duration of each one of your peaks.

COMPARISONS

If the number of one of your pinnacles appears in the chart set up with the full baptismal name and birthdate, it has a special significance.

Example:

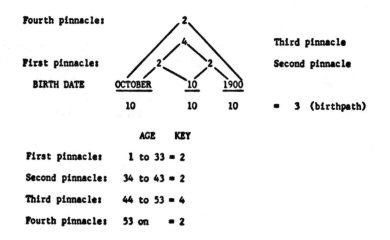

Fourth pinnacle:

First pinnacle:

BIRTH DATE

	AGE	KEY
First pinnacle:	1 to 33	= 2
Second pinnacle:	34 to 43	= 2
Third pinnacle:	44 to 53	= 4
Fourth pinnacle:	53 on	= 2

Figure 11-1

Example·

Richard Burton, the actor, was born on November 10, 1925.

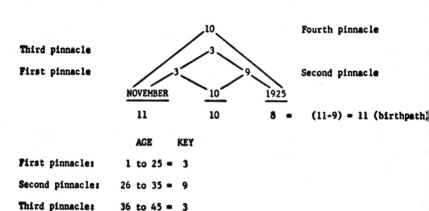

	AGE	KEY
First pinnacle:	1 to 25	= 3
Second pinnacle:	26 to 35	= 9
Third pinnacle:	36 to 45	= 3
Fourth pinnacle:	46 on	= 10

Figure 11-2

For Example:

1. If your ambition or soul urge number and your pinnacle number are indentical, then opportunities or events will present themselves to realize your desire.

2. If your destiny number and your pinnacle number are the same, then you will receive help to carry out the work of your talents or abilities.

3. If the number of your birthpath and your pinnacle number are identical, not only will opportunities for your activities be provided for you, but you will find it an easy period to learn the lessons required of you.

4. If your pinnacle number is the same as your karmic lesson, it then will be a difficult period unless you have previously learned your lesson.

5. If your pinnacle and your power numbers are alike, then success should be imminent for you if you utilize your potentials fully.

TABLE OF MEANINGS OF YOUR PINNACLES

One

The *one* pinnacle gives you the opportunity to be a leader, for you have executive ability, are individualistic in thought and action, independent, and original. This and a ten pinnacle often force you to stand on your own feet, and rely only upon yourself and not others for success. If this occurs as a first pinnacle, it may be a difficult period for you, for a young person is not always prepared to be courageous and independent, and so you will often lose the great opportunity provided to use original ideas. It might even make you obstinate and domineering. As a latter pinnacle, it will give you the chance to do outstanding work. It is always an active period filled with changes.

Two

The number *two* pinnacle demands cooperation and diplomacy. It often entails partnerships, as it is better for you to work with or for others than in an individual capacity. Patience is also being tested, for haste makes waste under a two. This is not a period to be independent, for harmony with, and the ability to get along with others, is important. You may feel very sensitive during this period, but you should be careful not to show your feelings. You work well in detail, collecting, or sharing with others. Difficulties in partnerships (even marriage) may crop up. If an eleven occurs as your pinnacle, a dissolution of a partnership (marriage or business) may take place, which may cause you to seek solace in religion or spiritual studies.

Three

This is a good period to develop your creative or artistic ability, as you are inspirational and have good ideas. It is not a physical, but a mental period. You may have the opportunity for writing, speaking, interior designing, and stage or movie entertainment. Your imagination and feeling will be on top. This is also an excellent period to attract money. As a first pinnacle the advantage of the three can be ignored, for few young individuals are serious-minded enough to put forth the effort necessary to channel their talent in a definite artistic or creative field. The emotions should be curbed at all times and kept under control.

Four

Under a *four* pinnacle it is expedient to lay a good foundation for the future, but hard work will be required of you. This is a practical period which may not be easy to face, as it demands constant service and effort. This is an excellent time to save and accumulate a bank account for future needs. If a *four* occurs as a *first* pinnacle, it means that your childhood will be a serious and demanding one. You may be forced to go to work early to earn a living. This pinnacle is one of maintaining order, and of systematizing, detailing, and building by placing ideas and facts in definite order. Your family may be a huge responsibility or duty. Practicing economy will be a requirement. It can be a welcome period, for you have a chance to put your ideas into practical form.

Five

While this is a period of freedom for you, you must be willing to let go of the old and accept changes. You will experience restlessness, change, and uncertainty, as this is not a time to stay at home and relax. A *five* pinnacle demands versatility, activity, public life, and much experience, for this is a time of advancement and progress. Money will be fluctuating, sometimes plentiful and other times scarce. You will have an opportunity for civic interests, advertising, selling, and a new phase of life. You may be forced to adapt to new friends and environment, but you should not try to act impulsively. This is an active period and not one of retirement.

Six

The *six* pinnacle is centered around many duties and responsibilities, especially in the home, for you may have the care of children, relatives, or of property. It gives you a chance to be useful, cultivate love, and serve willingly. You may go beyond the home and serve humanity. You can make money, but this requires much work and settling down. This is not a pinnacle for personal interests solely. Happiness results from giving and helping others as well as your own family circle. The *six* gives you love and protection through the family. It is a good final pinnacle as it may bring reward for your efforts, financial success, and happiness. You may marry during this pinnacle if you are single, for you will have the opportunity to do so now. It will be good.

Seven

Under a *seven* pinnacle you should be interested in educational and scientific pursuits. You should specialize, as perfection is demanded. This is a good period to study metaphysics and the hidden forces of nature. You will be interested in spiritual progress, and not material success during this period. You may become aloof, introspective, feel repressed, and be moody, which may cause trouble in your family. You may feel you lack money, but if you study, train your mind, learn, and develop a good understanding of the meaning of life, your knowledge and skill will bring success in the long run. You must be honest, patient, and understanding, otherwise you may have difficulty in marriage or in any partnership.

Eight

This is an excellent period for you financially. You can obtain a position of authority and fame through exercising good judgment.

While this is an excellent pinnacle for material gain, it is not an easy one, as it demands strength, courage, ambition, and constant effort. Laziness and lack of ambition are not tolerated under this influence. You may go into business early in life. A large expenditure of money may be necessary to maintain an undertaking under this pinnacle. You may experience many problems due to trusting the wrong people, or relying on luck. Good judgment, and a thorough understanding of others based on sound principles rather than feeling, is essential. You can be an outstanding person if you work unceasingly.

Nine

This is a pinnacle of completion. If you have learned to be impersonal, selfless, and universal in your outlook, not aiming for personal love or friendships, then this will be a rewarding pinnacle. This period can bring you beauty, art, and philanthropy. Much compassion, tolerance, and living for others is expected of you. This is a difficult pinnacle, as few have learned to love and give without expecting any return. If you are resentful or selfish, then this will be an unhappy time. If *nine* is the *first* pinnacle, a divorce or unhappy love affair may occur, but this often ends up a blessing. This is an excellent period to attract money and success, if you have aimed high enough to work for the good of mankind and not for yourself. Money can be lost, but it will be gained again. As a number nine, you will be tested constantly for your compassion and love of others. If it occurs as a *second* or *third* pinnacle, many emotional experiences will crop up.

Eleven

The *eleven* pinnacle will give you the opportunity of being in the limelight and appearing before the public. This is a good period for spiritual expansion. You may be living under much nervous tension as much is expected of you, and your ideals should be above average. This is a good period for fame, illumination, and inspiration. You may be led to uncover inventive ability or religious tendencies.

Twenty-two

This is a period where materialism and idealism are combined. It covers a wide field of endeavor, and may bring you greatness.

Under the twenty-two master pinnacle, which is the highest obtainable, you may be interested in promoting national or international affairs, for you will be able to see over large fields of expansion. Very few individuals are privileged to experience this pinnacle, for few have evolved to the extent to meet its demands. You must think big and for the benefit of the world while living under this powerful pinnacle.

TWELVE

How You Can Apply the Cosmic Alphabet to Understand Your Numbers Better

The plan for our digit system follows a definite sequence. To maintain order, names or numbers had to be established. They reveal the scientific foundation for our numbering system. After you have learned the reason for the specific succession of symbols or numbers, you will readily see that they had to follow their exact order. Just as in the case of building a house you must first place the foundation before erecting the sidewalls and roof, numbers evolved into their present position because of necessity. They follow the evolution or growth of individuals.

After studying the aspects of each number in their exact sequence, you will have a better understanding of the basic principle behind your own numbers when you set up your chart, analyze the numbers, and interpret their meaning.

THE PLAN FOR BUILDING AND INTERPRETING THE COSMIC ALPHABET

Number 0

 In the beginning (going to be) our world or universe was a nebulous mass or ball whirling at its own rate of vibration. It had no beginning and no ending, signifying eternity, and it resembled a circle or cipher. A zero or circle is the embryo of all numbers. Since there was no life or action upon this universe, there was no motivation. When a seed (or life force) was planted in the circle, it

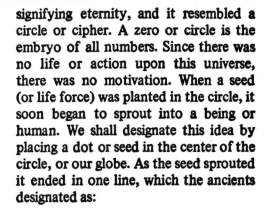

soon began to sprout into a being or human. We shall designate this idea by placing a dot or seed in the center of the circle, or our globe. As the seed sprouted it ended in one line, which the ancients designated as:

Number 1. Monad ... Unity

Number One stands for man, or the masculine principle. It is the symbol of the Sun, and it is the father of numbers or unity. The savage pointed to himself indicating the ME or ONE principle by placing one stick in the sand. One stands alone. It is creative, engendering originality and leadership. It suggests the source of ideas, and indicates man's first awareness of himself.

Number 2. Dyad ... Duality

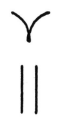

Many years later the savage evolved sufficiently to realize he had a mate. He designated this idea by pointing first to himself (ME) and then to his mate (MINE or YOU). He represented this principle by placing two sticks in the sand, indicating two ones. Another symbol which he used for this idea was the two wings of a bird.

Number 3. Triad ... Trinity

The result of man and his mate procreating was the offspring or the child.

Three is the expression of one and two. Now man had to find a symbol to include all three of them. He portrayed this by drawing a triangle, or a three lined figure, forming the first closed plane or the family circle. It is the first perfect number or trinity, and it is of spiritual significance. Three means completion. Another symbol with which man designated this idea was a three leaf clover, and another, two semi-circles.

Number 4. Tetrad ... Foundation

After man realized he had a mate and a child it became imperative that he provide shelter and protection for them. This meant building a dwelling or foundation. Four is a material number. Man stated this idea in several ways. He drew a square of four lines. This symbol is concrete, down-to-earth, and suggests a solid foundation, and much hard work requiring efficiency. Another symbol which the ancients used was a man holding up a triangle, while another symbol consisted of drawing four animal legs. The square symbolizes life or the idea of a universal plan.

Number 5. Pentad ... Adventure

Having provided his family with a place to live, man now felt he had earned the right to look around and enjoy himself. This included curiosity about life and sex, the five senses, travel, and change. He became an adventurer reaching out in five directions. Man symbolized this idea by drawing a five-pointed-star, and also by pointing to the five fingers of one hand.

Number 6. Hexad . . . Domesticity

After satiating his curiosity, man now was ready to build a home and take an interest in community life. The difference between building a house (4), and a home (6) is that the latter includes love, marriage, compassion, and an interest in others. Early man suggested this idea by drawing two triangles or six lines, indicating two closed figures. Another symbol for this was man standing beside a family circle.

Number 7. Heptad . . . Perfection

Having been supplied with love, a home, and a family, man was now ready from the evolutionary standpoint to become interested in spiritual progress. This was designated by placing the triangle of spirit over the square of matter, making seven lines. The square of four lines is solid and down-to-earth, while the triangle of three is creative and inspirational.

Number 8. Og-do-ad . . . Expansion

Having had time to develop his spiritual nature, man now concentrated on physical expansion and big business leading to worldly success. He designated this by placing one circle above the other, or two squares of four lines each placed over one another. Eight represents hard work and expansion in the material world.

Number 9. Ennaed . . . Humanity

The nine came into being when man became enough of a humanitarian to be interested in helping his neighbor. This he revealed by drawing man (1) holding up the world or circle. Also the triple triangle carried the same message. Now he had run the whole gamut of emotions and experiences.

WHAT YOUR AGE DIGIT CAN DO FOR YOU

Your age digit is an additional force which will guide you in meeting your experiences in making decisions. All of you have responsibilities, the extent of which is determined by your numerological age.

HOW TO FIGURE YOUR AGE DIGIT

You should follow the calendar year from January to January. Let's imagine that the universal calendar day is March 1, 1972. You are twenty-three years of age and will remain so until your birthday on October 1, 1972, at which time you will become twenty-four. You will be both twenty-three and twenty-four in 1972. Your age digit for the year 1972 will be:

$$\frac{23}{5} \quad + \quad \frac{24}{6} = 11$$

Your age digit for 1972 will be *eleven*. Look at the table page 123 for an explanation of the two. After your birthday in October until the end of the year, the six of the twenty-four will be more effective, although the 11 (2) of the entire year will operate until January 1, 1973. In 1973 you will be both:

$$\frac{24}{6} \quad + \quad \frac{25}{7} = 13 = 4$$

Your age digit for 1973 will be *four*.

Now figure your own age digit. Then turn to the following table for an explanation of the significance of your age digits for your personal guidance.

TABLE OF AGE DIGITS AND THEIR MEANINGS

Digit No. Meaning

1. Always shows new interests, new ideas, new occupations.
2. A tricky vibration which can be limiting or inspirational. It usually indicates a change of residence, business, or partnership.
3. Social or artistic beginning in a new field, the type of which is indicated by the dominant influence (personal year). Avoid emotional confusion.
4. Indicates routine rather than action. Put affairs in order. Shows change in business or domestic routine over which you have no control.
5. Points to social or artistic change. Good for selling or short trips.
6. Changes in the home, often leading to divorce or separation.

Digit No. Meaning

Advise careful thought before acting. Shows domesticity.
7. Marriage vibration for a female . . . finances for a male. Good time for occult study, meditation, introspection. Watch health and finances
8. Executive and business deals will be closed satisfactorily. Good time to buy or sell property. Many delays will be experienced.
9. This marks a close of one period and an impending beginning in a new line, depending on dominant influence. Watch health. Loss possible.
11. Vibration of inspiration and peace. See also Number Two.
22. Indicates mastery. May travel across water. This number does not occur in an age digit.

YOUR LETTER TRANSITS—WHAT THEY MEAN TO YOU

The yearly or letter transit means that you live one year in the vibration of each letter of your original given name, beginning at your birth. In other words, in evaluating letter transits, you are under the influence of the first letter of your first name at birth depending on the value of that letter, and then you move on to the second letter for the duration of the number value of that letter. When you have transited the full name, then you have completed the name cycle. Then you begin again with the first letter of your first name. The last letter of the first name, and the last letter of the last name are critical years, especially for the aged.

Example:

ROBERT   BROWN

9 6 2 5 9 2   2 9 6 5 5

Robert will be transiting under the letter R (value nine) for the first nine years of his life. Then he will be under the influence of 0 for the next six years, at which time he will be fifteen years of age. Following this he will be under the vibration of B for the next two years, E for the following five years, R for the next nine years, and T for the following two years. He will be thirty-three years old when he has completed the letter transit of his first name (Robert) for the first time.

Now we will start with the last name of Brown. He will be under the vibration of B for the next two years, then R (nine years), 0 (six years), W (five years) and N (five years). He will be sixty years old when he has transited his complete name. He will begin his sixty-first year with the R of his first name.

TABLE OF VALUE OF LETTER TRANSITS

A, J, S, = 1 year's transit	F, O, X, = 6 year's transit
B, K, T, = 2 year's transit	G, P, Y, = 7 year's transit
C, L, U, = 3 year's transit	H, Q, Z, = 8 year's transit
D, M, V, = 4 year's transit	I, R, = 9 year's transit
E, N, W, = 5 year's transit	

WHY YOU MAY DIFFER FROM OTHERS WITH THE
SAME NUMERICAL VALUE

1. While *A, J, and S* all have the value of *one*, and are creators, leaders, and originators, there's a difference in their makeup. *A* is aggressive and will not be detoured from its goal. It, as well as the J are mental, but J may be inclined to put things off and so not complete the task. The S is more emotional, and consequently the feelings would enter into your approach, which might cloud your clear thinking.

2. *B, K, and T* all have the value of *two*. They are followers rather than leaders. B is shy, emotional, and needs affection and mothering. K is intuitive, and follows hunches. It is receptive. T is nervous and eager for spiritual development.

3. *C, L, and U* have the value of *three* and are interested in self-expression. They are social, and lean to the lighter side of life. C has psychic ability but is not cognizant of its gift. L is mental and uses reasoning power, while U is weaker than the others, and suffers because of its dual nature.

4. *D, M, V* have the value of *four*. They are down to earth and practical. D is efficient, a hard worker, and usually is not emotional. M is thorough like the D, but is repressed and unexpressive, and often is unfeeling toward others. V is inspirational and intuitive, and listens to his small voice within.

5. *E, N, and W* have the value of five. They are physical numbers and are often bound up in the senses. E, while physical, can reach the realm of inspiration. N is imaginative and wavering in decisions, though he uses mental power in his interpretations. W is also physical, and while desiring higher aspirations, is often remorseful because he cannot reach them.

6. *F, O, X* have the value of *six*. As such they are able to carry much responsibility, and are tied to home duties. F is intuitional but has a dual nature. He is a cross bearer. O is inspirational but inclined to draw power to himself. He gives out very little due to his conservative nature. X is the most difficult of the *sixes*, for this letter usually entails sactifice. It is a karmic letter.

7. *G, P, Y* have the value of *seven*. They are mental, analytical, and introspective. G is mental but aloof, and needs understanding to keep it from experiencing tragedy. P is also mental, but lacks the willpower of G. It is inexpressive and unsure of itself Y is dual

in nature. It has fine psychic gifts, but being dual it has difficulty choosing which way to go.

8. *H, Q, and Z* have the value of *eight*. They are the in between letters bridging consciousness. H is advancing from the material to the mental plane, but it is vacillating in decisions. Q functions in two worlds, and so can·be a dangerous power if lacking guidance. Z is inspirational and understands human emotions, being able to balance and control emotional crises.

9. *I and R* have a value of *nine*. They are selfless numbers interested in humanity. I is the light bearer. He may guide a lost soul or knife him, for he may be destructive. R is more selfless and understanding than any other number or letter.He is tolerant with others, but is often the goat, for others will take advantage of him.

Notice: While it is not important to know the letter transits to figure a numeroscope, it does give additional insight into character.

THIRTEEN

How to Tell What Type of Individual You Really Are for Your Greatest Success

There are four planes of consciousness or expression by which you reveal your personality, characteristics, skill, and general disposition. They are:

1. Mental
2. Physical
3. Emotional
4. Intuitive

The degree of balance between them will indicate not only what type of individual you really are, but in which field of activity or expression you will do your best work. The plane to which you bring the most experience and knowledge is your greatest asset in the matter of a vocation. It will guide you in deciding whether you should pursue a business, creative, scientific, or artistic career. From your planes of expression or temperament you will learn whether you have a practical, emotional, or imaginative outlook on life. However, you must remember to consult your destiny and birthpath for the last word in selecting a vocation.

THE NATURE OF PLANES OF TEMPERAMENT

The Planes of Temperament show the disposition or nature of an individual—the way he will express himself—how he will handle responsibility—and how he will reveal his character and skills. In other words, the planes give the true state of mind of an individual.

PLANES OF TEMPERAMENT

MENTAL   = mind . . . reasoning power, thought

PHYSICAL   = body . . . practicality, materiality, form

EMOTIONAL   = heart . . . emotions, feelings imagination

INTUITIONAL = spirit . . . intuition, inner guidance

ANALYSES OF THE PLANES YOU MAY FUNCTION ON

1. *The Mental Plane* indicates your mind or reasoning power. If you have many numbers on this plane, you are equipped to handle business enterprises on a large scale. You have the ability to reason, analyze, gather facts, and weigh them carefully, for you will not accept facts unless they can be proven. You represent will and determination, and have an excellent mind for leadership, logic, and efficient deductions. You may turn to invention, international affairs, or become a technical writer. Too many numbers on this plane may show you to be too headstrong and unreasonable. It may even affect your health.

2. *The Physical Plane* represents your body, or material objects which have form and practicality. If you have many numbers on this plane, you are economical, and are governed by system and order. You have the gift of concentration. Being down to earth, you prefer facts rather than rely on your imagination and ideas, for you have the common sense touch. You represent the builder, worker, and economist. If you are low on physical numbers, it means you can't be depended upon for a true sense of values and practicality. Many physical numbers show you have great endurance, for you are capable of doing hard work. A lack of physical numbers could also show delicate health, while an abundance of them shows that if you are ill, you can pull through repeatedly and recover.

3. *The Emotional Plane* is governed by your emotions or feelings. You are more heart than mind. Many numbers on the emotional plane show you are sympathetic and sentimental, and that love and affection rule over reason and logic. You have a great

imagination, and are artistic and creative, but you are absorbed in ideas rather than material facts. Few numbers show it is hard for you to express your feelings. Too many show your lack of self-direction, also that you are high-strung.

4. *The Intuitive Plane* signifies that you are more on the spiritual level of thinking than on the practical or physical plane. Your actions will be based on understanding and wisdom, rather than on hard facts. Being guided by inner knowing, you draw on the spiritual for your understanding on all the other planes. You are capable of great analysis, technical facts, and insight into the feelings of others. Many numbers on this plane indicate ability in either literature, religion, invention, or prophecy, but not according to the normal way of thinking and actions. The intuitive plane promotes tolerance, reverence, compassion, kindliness, prophecy, and inner guidance. You may be plagued with delicate health.

NUMBERS RELATING TO DEFINITE PLANES

MENTAL PLANE   On the mental plane are all *ones* and *eights* (1 and 8)

PHYSICAL PLANE   On the physical are all *fours* 'and *fives* (4 and 5)

EMOTIONAL PLANE   On the emotional are all *twos, threes,* and *sixes* (2,3,6)

INTUITIVE PLANE   On the intuitive are all *sevens* and *nines* (7 and 9)

MEANING OF THE NUMBERS

Numbers One and Eight

(1 and 8). If you have many number *ones* and *eights,* you are on the mental plane and represent mind qualities.

One is an independent thinker, originator, and a leader. However, he may have strong likes and dislikes. He could be opinionated and bored.

Eight is governed by logic and reason. He has executive ability, and is ambitious for power. He likes to make a good showing, as he has much pride. He's always striving for the betterment of himself. He likes to be the boss, and does not follow orders readily.

Numbers Four and Five

(4 and 5). If you have many number *fours* and *fives*, you are on the physical plane.

Fours are practical, efficient, hard workers, and can be depended upon for responsibility. They are not creative, for they have very little imagination. They may be argumentative since they are not amenable to new ideas.

Fives are adventurous and inquisitive, but they are not as practical as the fours. They like change, the unusual, new things, and original ideas.

Fives are restless when forced to do routine work. As active individuals, they are promoters and natural salesmen.

Numbers Two, Three, and Six

(2, 3, 6). If you have many number *twos*, *threes*, and *sixes*, you are on the emotional plane.

Twos represent feeling and imagination, for they are very sensitive. They like detail, collecting facts, and all forms of beauty. Since they lack self-confidence, they should be in partnership with another and not own their own business. They are subject to worry, fear, and a feeling of inadequacy. They are musical and spiritual.

Threes are very artistic, and they have considerable talent for using words in writing or speaking. Many *threes* have a tendency to be disorderly and unsystematic. They do not like to be tied down to pure facts, as their imaginations are strong. They are very creative, but they act impulsively at times. Being versatile, they are apt to scatter their talents. Threes are not at their best doing manual labor. They can make others happy, for they are entertainers.

Sixes can carry much responsibility. They can be depended upon to follow through with plans. They are artistic but practical. They need a home and family, and are good disciplinarians. They are also interested in community and welfare work. Negative aspects of a *six* are that they can be demanding and domineering. Because they try to insist that others live up to their ideals, they often fail to gain the affection they strongly desire. *Sixes* may experience many difficulties through their children.

Numbers Seven and Nine

(7, 9). If you have many number *sevens* and *nines,* you are on the intuitive or spiritual plane.

Sevens are psychic, analytical, and use E.S.P (Extrasensory Perception) or intuition for guidance. They are excellent in scientific affairs. *Sevens* are reserved, refined, and dignified. They are not very friendly or socially inclined. They demand perfection for themselves and from others. *Sevens* can be critical, sarcastic, and show considerable temper. *Sevens* delve into the hidden forces of nature.

Nines are very deep thinkers. They can work with all people. They are dramatically inclined. While they are impersonal, they can become distressed if they fail to get love and approval, for they like to appeal to the crowd and be admired. *Nines* are usually tolerant, sympathetic, and generous. They need guidance, for they are often dreamers.

HOW TO SET UP AN ANALYSIS

Now let's set up a sample name so that you will know how to find on which plane you have the most numbers. For example let's work the following name:

C A M E R O N   R I C H A R D   D A V I D S O N

3 1 4 5 9 6 5   9 9 3 8 1 9 4   4 1 4 9 4 1 6 5

First you add the number of ones in his full name, then the twos, etc. going through all nine numbers. Tabulate your findings thus:

No. of ones 4
No. of twos 0
No. of threes 2
No. of fours 5
No. of fives 3
No. of sixes 2
No. of sevens 0
No. of eights 1
No. of nines 5

On the mental plane Cameron Richard Davidson has four (1's) and one (8) = 5.

On the physical plane he has five (4's) and three (5's) = 8.

On the emotional plane he has no (2's); two (3's), and two (6's) = 4.

On the intuitive plane he has no (7's) and five (9's) = 5.

Most individuals are average and well-balanced, operating on all planes of expression, for they have some qualities of each plane. When a person has a zero or a low number on a plane, it simply means that he is not outstanding in that field, but that his strength lies in some other plane of temperament. If an individual has great extremes, then we can look for a strange person who may be unorthodox. A genius is often unbalanced, for he may have too many numbers on the intuitive plane and few or none on the physical.

Mr. Davidson is functioning primarily on the physical plane with five *fours* and three *fives*. However, he has great imagination and mentality with four *ones* to carry out his aspirations. He is not ruled by emotions, for he sticks to material facts. He is not psychic. He likes to be with people, and needs and wants their approval. With five *nines* he is dramatically inclined, and can be quite impersonal in his dealings with others. He is practical and dependable. Since he has many numbers on this plane, it shows he's capable of doing hard work.

We'll set another name for analysis. Get your pencil and analyze the following well-known name:

D WI G H T   D A V I D   E I S E N H O W E R

4 5 9 7 8 2   4 1 4 9 4   5 9 1 5 5 8 6 5 5 9

No. of ones	2
No. of twos	1
No. of threes	0
No. of fours	4
No. of fives	6
No. of sixes	1
No. of sevens	1
No. of eights	2
No. of nines	4

On the mental plane he has two (1's) and two eights (8's) = 4.
On the physical plane he has four (4's) and six (5's) = 10.

On the emotional plane he has one (2); no (3's); and one (6) = 2.

On the intuitive plane he has four (9's) and one (7) = 5.

Mr. Eisenhower, former president of the United States, shows ten (10) numbers on the physical plane. When any person has as many as ten on this plane it indicates that his name will be known before the public at some period in his life. He fulfilled this requirement both in the military service as a General, and in the political field as President. Dwight Eisenhower, from his many numbers on the the physical plane, shows that he had a gift of common sense, as he was always down-to-earth and very practical. He was systematic and orderly, and had the ability to work hard, be economical (even his eighty dollar coffin he wanted to be buried in shows this), and was interested in humanity. When ill, he was able on a number of occasions to recover, showing great endurance physically. He was not governed or swayed by his emotions (2), but did rely on his intuition (5) to guide him in major decisions.

Now set up your own name to learn on which plane you are chiefly functioning. By means of this chapter you can write a description of your salient points. In seeking a position, it is important to know what type you are, and in which plane you will be most successful. Forewarned is forearmed!

Universal Years, Months, and Days: How They Influence You

You, as well as everybody and everything in the entire universe, move in a definite cycle, but you have your own rate of *vibration*. At the end of twelve months, a new year, or universal cycle begins, and each year has a different influence depending on one of the nine digits to which it reduces. This number indicates the type of events or activity you can look for the world to be launching. Universal year cycles belong to everyone alike, while personal cycles apply to you as an individual.

UNIVERSAL YEARS

You must follow the calendar year from January to January in figuring the universal years, days, and months. To find the universal vibration for any year, you add the single digits of the prevailing year together and reduce these to a final digit.

Example:

The *vibration* for the year 1972 is one, because 1972 reduces to one, namely:

$$(1 + 9 + 7 + 2 = 19 = 10 = 1)$$

The year 1973 will be a *two* year, etc.

134

TABLE OF UNIVERSAL YEARS
VIBRATIONS AND THEIR MEANINGS

Vibration 1

A year of new events or achievements, especially in engineering, aviation, or invention. There will be much creative activity. A pioneering spirit and progressive plans will be much in evidence. A change is indicated.

Vibration 2

A year of peace and tranquility. Group work will be predominant. This is a year when tact and diplomacy are required. Agreements will be signed, and many statistics collected. Governmental work and politics will be in the foreground.

Vibration 3

A year when social life is uppermost in the minds of most individuals. There will be expansion in theaters and places of entertainment. A restlessness and recklessness will be noticeable. There may be a tendency for you to scatter your talents.

Vibration 4

A year to settle down to hard work. Thrift and economy must be practiced after living high last year. Building a good foundation is necessary. Jobs will be scarce, but progress will be made in manufacturing and education.

Vibration 5

A year of expansion, new interests, curiosity, change, versatility, and activity. Interest may lean toward metaphysics, psychology, or the occult sciences. A rejuvenation will be felt with better working conditions than in a four year period. Numerology and Astrology will flourish.

Vibration 6

An increase in marriages will take place. A year which is devoted to love and interest in the home and family circle. An advance in education and health conditions will be noticeable. Many club houses, schools, and new homes will be built.

Vibration 7

This is a vibration of perfection and analysis instead of expansion. It usually is a good financial year, especially for those engaged in agriculture and mining pursuits. A spiritual wave will be felt, and many will meditate and turn inward for solace.

Vibration 8

A year of big business expansion, progress, and prosperity. Engineering projects should boom. Relationships with foreign countries should be profitable. Thinking should be done on a large scale.

Vibration 9

A vibration of love for mankind, in which selfless service should be paramount. This is an excellent year to give your business a general house-cleaning, and finish up odds and ends. You must learn to let go of the old and cultivate tolerance, understanding, and love.

Vibration 11

A master year governed by idealism and inspiration. Religious interests will boom, and people will be interested in Occultism, Spiritualism, and Evangelism. Revival meetings will be crowded. Psychology will be a major subject of discussion. This is a good year for promotional affairs, although business may not be paramount in the minds of individuals.

Vibration 22

Another master year, but this has a worldly impetus. It will be both idealistic and materialistic. This year brings greatness in business expansion, and a strong humanitarian force. There will be an· aim toward world betterment rather than just community progress. The year 1975 reduces to 22, and it should have far reaching effects in material and spiritual affairs.

UNIVERSAL VIBRATIONS OF MONTHS

In order to find the universal *month*, you add the number of the calendar month to the number of the universal year. The value of the months follow the calendar.
Thus:

January	= 1	July	= 7
February	= 2	August	= 8
March	= 3	September	= 9
April	= 4	October	= 10 or 1
May	= 5	November	= 11 or 2
June	= 6	December	= 12 or 3

To get the vibration of the month of March 1972 you add:

March   1972

3   +   1   =   4

March 1972 will be a *four* month.

The universal month is influenced by the universal year, but each month gives a different aspect to the year.

WHAT THE UNIVERSAL MONTHS INDICATE

1. Leadership, new ideas, progress originality.
2. Peace, cooperation, collection, politics, details.
3. Entertainment, creation, joy, activity.
4. Self-discipline, schedule, hard work, building a foundation.
5. Travel, sales, advertising, sports, speculation, enthusiasm.
6. Community affairs, weddings, health, beauty, food, home.
7. Intuition, analysis, improved finances, quietude, invention.
8. Organization, business expansion, corporations, enterprises.
9. Completion, elimination, progress, understanding.
11. Spirituality, electricity, aviation, Evangelism.
22. National and international projects, politics, railroads, improvements.

UNIVERSAL VIBRATIONS OF DAYS

Just as each individual has a different rate of vibration, each day of the year has its own rate. Some days are auspicious or favorable for seeking a new position, while others would be more profitably spent at home working, or in studying or resting. Still other days lend themselves best for entertainment. The days which fall in your own concord are usually the most advantageous for you. If your birthday falls in the air or artistic concord of 3, 6, and 9 the days which harmonize with any of these numbers or add up or reduce to these numbers, will be favorable for you. If your birthday is in the water or scientific concord of 1, 5, and 7, any which harmonize with these will be good, while if you belong in the fire or business concord of 2, 4, 8, 11, and 22, days which harmonize with these would be advantageous for you.

To get the universal vibration for a certain day, you add the month, day, and year of that date and reduce them .

Example:

November	6	1972	
2	6	1	= 9

November is the eleventh month. We add this to the day, which is six, and the year, which is one. November 6, 1972 will be a nine day, a time to finish up odds and ends. It is not an auspicious day to start anything new. It would be favorable for those whose birthdays fall on any numbers which can be reduced to 3, 6, or 9, such as the 12th, 15th, or 27th.

VIBRATION TABLE OF UNIVERSAL DAYS

Following is a table of vibrational influences by days:

1. Aggression is the keynote. Action, determination, and strikes may be promoted. Sell yourself or your idea. Make a change by starting something new.
2. Cooperation is the keynote. Be quiet and collect material. Use diplomacy and tact. There will be an increase in deaths.

3. Self-expression is the keynote. This is a sociable day—good for entertainment. Visit beauty parlors, the theatre, or a dance hall. Activity and nervous energy will be paramount.

4. Hard work is the keynote. This is a day to devote to routine, details, thrift, and scheduling of your affairs. Markets will be steady. Illnesses and strikes may occur.

5. Enthusiasm is the keynote. This is a day of freedom, change, and curiosity. Push sales, speculate, travel, and be active.

6. Domesticity is the keynote. Eat at home instead of in public restaurants. Avoid arguments. Watch your health and education. Start to build a new home, or sign a lease.

7. Perfection is the keynote. Spend a quiet day at home or in the country. Mining stocks may climb. This is an excellent day to draw up a will.

8. Organization is the keynote. Sign big contracts, invest in stocks, and hold directors' meetings. This a day where business and executive ability will shine. Cooperate with others.

9. Good will is the keynote. Arrange to give a speech today. National advertising will be effective. Selflessness, tolerance, brotherly love, and achievement are on the agenda. Business can be conducted as advantageously by telephone or telegraph as by personal contact.

11. Promotion is the keynote. Be in the limelight. This is a day of illumination, inspiration, and vision. It has the qualities of two, but with more leadership. Promote engineering, television, aviation, and electricity today. Eleven is a spiritual day.

22. Internationalism is the keynote. This is a good day for those in politics or governmental work such as ambassadors. International and national projects will be in the foreground. International improvements will be noticeable. Twenty-two has the qualities of four, but it has far greater effects. While this is a material day, inspiration is required to put over big deals.

FIFTEEN

The Influence of Your Personal Years, Months, and Days

In addition to the universal year, month, and day, vibrational influences in Chapter 14 which affect everyone alike, you have a *personal* year, month, and day which affect you individually. Your personal year offers you certain opportunities, and a chance to develop along the lines suggested in these vibrations. If you miss the favorable vibration available in a one year, you'll have to wait nine years for the cycle to return to a one year in order to get equally advantageous effects from a similar vibration to start something new, be creative, and work independently.

HOW TO FIND WHAT TYPE OF WORK YOU SHOULD DO IN YOUR PERSONAL YEAR

The number of your personal year will show what type of work. you should do in that year to develop yourself and make the most of your experiences, and so achieve harmony and satisfactory results.

Since the cycle is intertwined with the pinnacle in operation at that time, you can analyze it without resorting to fortune-telling to find what is likely to happen, and what you should do to prepare yourself for the demands of the personal year and the requirements of the pinnacles.

YOUR PERSONAL YEAR

You must know the current or universal year before you can determine what is your personal year.

140

To find your personal year, add the digit of your month and your day of birth to the present or universal year (omitting your own year of birth).

Example:

Your birthdate is January 26, 1918. You want to find your personal year for 1971. The universal year is *nine:*

(1 + 9 + 7 + 1 = 18 = 9)

MONTH	DAY	YEAR (Universal)
January	26	1971
1	8	9

Now add the month (1) plus the day (8) plus the year (9) = 18 = 9. Your personal year for 1971 is *nine.* In this case it is the same as the universal year. Your personal year for 1972, as well as your universal year, will be 10 = 1. This means that 1972 should have a double effect of the one for you. It would be an excellent year for starting something new. If you have had plans for a change of positions or a home, now is the time to do so. If you want to start a new business project, 1972 would be a good year to launch it. While the universal year is also one, and affects everyone as an active and productive year, it would affect you especially, since it is both your personal and universal year.

Now let's figure another personal year. Let's imagine you were born on June 23, 1934, and you want to know what your personal year is for 1972. To find this, you add your personal month, (which is June = 6) and your personal day (23) to the universal year of 1972, which is one.

Thus:

JUNE	23	1972
6	5	19
		10
6 +	5 +	1 = 12 = 3

Your personal year for 1972 is three, while the universal year is one. It will be a social and enjoyable year for you personally (3). This would be a good year to give speeches, entertain, and write. See table on page 142 for additional information.

TABLE OF PERSONAL YEARS

Vibration 1

You are entering a new cycle, which will last for the next nine years. A one year is excellent to start something new or to make the change about which you have been undecided. Be individual, and do not be afraid to specialize or promote new ideas. You must learn to stand on your own feet, for success will come only through your individual efforts. Resolve to be a leader and a pioneer. If you are comtemplating a change in positions, now is the time to apply for the new job. This year requires work, organization, and clear thinking, not relaxation.

Vibration 2

You will gain more this year by staying in the background and waiting for things to come to you. Patience, diplomacy, and tact will be necessary in dealing with others. Partnerships, agreements and new friends may come if you are cooperative, friendly, quiet, and peaceful. You should collect and assort for future use, but do not push ahead as this may cause more delays. Plans of last year must have time to mature. Knowledge accumulated this year will be a great asset next year, when you will have the time and the opportunity to express yourself. Be unselfish and willing to share with others.

Vibration 3

Creativity, inspiration, and imagination are waiting to express themselves. Lecturing and writing will prove beneficial for you. You must exert considerable effort to put your ideas into reality. Since this is a social year, you may be inclined to drift along and merely enjoy yourself. Be selective in choosing companions. A good sense of humor will bring friendships and happiness in return for your efforts in wise self-expression. You may travel for pleasure, and also accumulate money.

Vibration 4

After last year's time for entertainment, now is the year to be practical, to stick your nose to the grindstone to carry out the plans and ideas instigated last year. Details, system, and order are paramount this year. You may have to attend to your health or that of someone in your family. You must also face other responsibilities such as handling property, being thrifty, and dealing in merchandising. All success comes through being economical and practical rather than depending on luck to progress materially.

Vibration 5

You will now feel a restlessness which may lead you to make some definite changes. Replacing the old with new ideas is good, but hastiness often causes future regrets. Freedom is uppermost in your mind. This is a favorable year for taveling, moving, or doing something different. Be sure to advertise your product. This can be an exciting year filled with variety, change, and progress.

Vibration 6

After last year's freedom, your interests will now be centered in the home and community. You will face many domestic responsibilities and duties. Love and service should be your paramount interest. If you give love and sympathy, you will receive them. This is a good year to build or buy a home, marry, or engage in a community project. You may even accumulate money, especially if you gladly accept obligations, and not be resentful or consider them a burden.

Vibration 7

You may be inclined to specialize, study, and follow intellectual pursuits, for this is a period for a mental housecleaning. You may want to be alone to meditate and aim for spiritual advancement. This is not a year for business expansion or for starting new things, but put the finishing touches to what was begun earlier. This may be a good financial year if you do not rush out after money.

Intuition plays an important part in your life, and this should help you understand yourself and others better. It can even bring recognition to you if you reason things out and deal fairly with all.

Vibration 8

Now is the time to reap the harvest sown in a one year. Big opportunities for advancement are yours if you work hard and push matters to a conclusion. Good judgment and efficiency in business will also be necessary. You may have to exert considerable effort and mental strain. Organization, planning, efficiency, and a businesslike attitude are essential. Remember this is a year of action. Avoid letting your emotions or sentiment gain an upper hand in your dealings, but face facts. You may have to let go of some things, but this may be good in the long run.

Vibration 9

You should finish up odds and ends and be willing to let go of old things. You are closing the nine year cycle, and are getting ready for new experiences. You may encounter losses in business and friendships unless you live impersonally. You must be tolerant, compassionate and forgiving. Then you will reap the reward of love, understanding, and wisdom. Watch your health this year.

Vibration 11

This is a master year. Unless you live up to its fullest requirements it reverts to a two, which may tie you up with details. This is a year of inspiration and psychic illumination. It could put you in the limelight, and even bring fame, if you follow your intuition and act on your hunches or ideas.

Vibration 22

The twenty-two master year brings universal appeal rather than anything personal. If not lived up to its possibilities, it reverts to a four, bringing hard work and limitations. The sky is the limit in a twenty-two year. It's a time to combine the inspirational and practical, and do big things for the benefit of humanity or the world, not merely for yourself or your community.

HOW TO ANALYZE YOUR PERSONAL MONTHS

To find your personal month, add the calendar month to your personal year. You will remember that you find the personal year by adding the month and day you were born to the universal or prevailing year. 1971 is a *nine* universal year. If you were born on June 9th of any year, you add the month (June = 6) to the day of your birth (9) plus the universal year (9) to get the personal year of *six* (6 + 9 + 9 = 24 = 6). Now we add the calendar month to the personal year. If you want to know what your personal month will be in April 1971 you add:

April (4) plus personal year (6) = 10 personal month.

While the universal month is *four* in April, your personal month will be *ten*. Look at the table for the interpretation. September, being a *nine* month, has the same vibration as the year.

TABLE OF VIBRATIONS OF PERSONAL MONTHS

Vibration   1. Action, creation, originality.
Vibration   2. Harmony, quietude, passivity.
Vibration   3. Entertainment, self-expression.
Vibration   4. Practicality, building a foundation, work.
Vibration   5. Change, freedom, new interests.
Vibration   6. Responsibilities, service, health, family love.
Vibration   7. Perfection, analysis, spiritual outlook.
Vibration   8. Vision, power, good judgment, business expansion.
Vibration   9. Philanthropy, selflessness, service.
Vibration 11. Illumination, idealism, religion, limelight.
Vibration 22. Materialism and idealism combined, worldly projects.

HOW TO ANALYZE YOUR PERSONAL DAYS

To find your personal day, add the calendar month and day to your personal year. For example, if your personal year is six and the calendar day and month are January 4th, your personal day will be:

Calendar month   =   January =   1

Calendar day   =   4

Personal year   =   _____6

                                     11

(Your personal day on January 4th.)

Now let's find the personal day for Albert Jones, born on November 3, 1933. The calendar day is January 15, 1972.

JANUARY   15,   1972

1   +   6   +   1   = 8

The universal day for him is *eight*. His personal year is November (11), plus 3 (day) plus universal year of 1 = 6. His personal day is: January (1) plus 15 (6) plus 6 (personal year) = (1 + 6 + 6 = 13 = 4). His personal day is 4, while the universal day is 8. While the universal day will benefit him as well as others, the personal day applies to him individually. He should concentrate on his work today (4), organizing the planning for the future. Being thrifty and practical (4), will show later good results. See table of personal days for further details.

TABLE OF PERSONAL DAYS

Vibration 1. Promote original ideas, sell self, be aggressive, do new things.
Vibration 2. Be cooperative, peaceful, receptive, collect and analyze details.
Vibration 3. Entertain, be gay, express yourself creatively, mingle in society.
Vibration 4. Be thrifty, organize and systematize work, work hard, concentrate.
Vibration 5. Be enthusiastic, travel, buy or sell, promote new ideas, act.
Vibration 6. Assume responsibilities in home and community, serve, avoid arguments.
Vibration 7. Follow hunch, rest, perfect what you started, concentrate.

Vibration   8. Sign big contracts, use tact and good judgment, invest in securities.

Vibration   9. Be selfless, express talents, promote love and brotherhood.

Vibration 11. Be a leader, promoter, shine in public, follow hunch, advertise.

Vibration 22. Be masterful and cooperative in big business, promote international projects.

Now figure your own personal year, month, and day following the instructions given previously in these chapters. Turn to the various tables for an explanation of each in structuring an analysis for your guidance for any goal you may wish to achieve.

SIXTEEN

The Karmic Law of Cause and Effect in Numerology

The power of Karma postulates the law of cause and effect. Everything that happens to you (effect) has had a previous cause.

The operation of Karmic law means that you can be the master of your own destiny.

HOW TO KNOW YOUR BARRIER TO SUCCESS

Your karmic lessons of life reflect qualities which you either lack or in which you are weak hindering your success. They indicate experiences or obligations which you avoided, or from which you managed to escape in some past life. They now crop up in your present life as barriers to your success unless you make a conscious effort to conquer them.

HOW TO FIND YOUR KARMIC MISSING NUMBERS

To determine what your karmic lessons are, you must set up your entire original name as given at birth. Any missing numbers in your name are experiences which you will meet, and which you should try to master. Occasionally your lack is supplied, or your difficulty overcome, when you change your name. However, you still must learn the lessons of your original name, and strengthen your character by realizing the necessity of definitely overcoming the weaknesses. If the missing number occurs in some other prominent place, such as your birthpath, soul's urge, destiny, or power number, then the karmic effect will be lessened, but the debt to your karmic destiny must still be paid.

Example:

MARTIN LUTHER KING

4 1 9 2 9 5   3 3 2 8 5 9   2 9 5 7

Analysis of Above Name

Number of:

1's	= 1	6's	= 0
2's	= 3	7's	= 1
3's	= 2	8's	= 1
4's	= 1	9's	= 4
5's	= 3		

The only missing digit in Martin Luther King's full original name is six, (see above 6's = 0) which means he had to learn to accept responsibility as a duty. He came into this world showing a previous lack in a former life of this desire. He also had no appreciation of beauty or the value of service, which he had to cultivate. His talents or strong points were four *nines*. Many *nines* show that he was primarily a peacemaker and humanitarian, working for the good of all. You will notice in his table that he had three twos and three fives. The fact that he showed three *fives* was inconsequential, for *five* is the number of man and it occurs in abundance in most charts. Therefore, it is best to deduct two from the total of five to get a true balance of that number Following is a table for your Karmic guidance.

NUMEROLOGY TABLE OF KARMIC LESSONS FOR GUIDANCE

Number 1

If you show few or no *ones*, you lacked initiative, ambition, originality, and independence in a past life. It means you do not think primarily of yourself. You show no domineering or aggressive qualities, but rather a fear or lack of trust in yourself. You dread making decisions or starting new things.

Number 2

If you show few or no *twos,* you lacked tact, diplomacy, and cooperation in the past. You fail to conserve time and save money. You are shy to the point of avoiding companions, but you now must learn to work with others, acquire patience, and attend to details.

Number 3

If you show few or no *threes,* you were unable to express yourself well in a former existence. You lack confidence in yourself, and would like to hide from the public. You also reveal a lack of imagination, a quick temper, and a scatterer of talents.

Number 4

If you show few of no *fours,* you formerly disliked hard work, attending to details, and being orderly. You must build a good foundation, not by avoiding work, but by patiently and slowly concentrating on the job and accepting no limitations.

Number 5

If you show few or no *fives,* you had a constant fear of facing change or anything new in a former life. A lack of understanding, curiosity, and interest in your fellowmen is indicated. This number is seldom lacking. Now you must learn to face change.

Number 6

If you show few or no *sixes,* you indicate an unwillingness to assume responsibility in the past. You fear being tied down to the care of a home and family. You have much to learn about being a good partner in marriage and a good parent, for many adjustments will be necessary, including domestic responsibility and service to others.

Number 7

If you show few or no *sevens*, you formerly lacked understanding between the material and spiritual, and an avoidance of turning within for guidance. You have a fear of faith and what it entails. You also disclose a lack of technique, analysis, and a willingness to train your mind to examine conditions before jumping to conclusions.

Number 8

If you show few or no *eights*, you lacked the ability or the efficiency to handle business or other material affairs. You must learn the value of money, and learn to organize and manage, for karma will force you to handle your own business.

Number 9

If you show few or no *nines* you lacked feeling and understanding. This means you will suffer many emotional upsets and disappointments until you have learned to be generous, sympathetic, loving, and interested in others.

TABLE OF NATURAL TALENTS
AND PERSONAL DEFICIENCIES

(Most frequent numbers)

Number

1 Many *ones* show ambition, independence, and individual interests. This often indicates a selfish, domineering person.

2 Many *twos* show tact and diplomacy. You are a lover of music, dancing, harmony, and color. You are able to cooperate with others.

Number

3 Many *threes* show you are able to express yourself well. You have a strong imagination, and a good sense of humor. You must learn to assume responsibility. Avoid being impatient.

4 Many *fours* show economy, thrift, order, honesty, and a penchant for hard work.

Number

You should learn to concentrate and use good judgment. You are good at details and routine. You may be stubborn.

5 Many *fives* show an interest in the opposite sex and the senses. You must guard against being impulsive and nervous. You should welcome change, travel, and excitement.

6 Many *sixes* show the ability to assume much responsibility. You are reliable, domestic, and a natural parent or teacher. You should avoid being agrumentative and quarrelsome.

Number

7 Many *sevens* show analysis, mental alertness, and a desire for perfection. You show poise and culture. If you have many *sevens*, you may be interested in metaphysical subjects, or be aloof.

8 Many *eights* show business ability. You could succeed in financial undertakings, for you have executive ability, and show leadership, initiative, tact, and a good sense of values.

9 Many *nines* show a universal outlook. You are artistic, and have creative and literary ability. You should enjoy traveling.

Now set up your own name and learn what you lack and must cultivate, as well as what your redeeming talents are.

MALIFIC OR KARMIC NUMBERS

How you can cancel their effects

Note that: Karmic numbers are not the same as Karmic lessons, which we discussed in full in the first part of this chapter. Not all individuals are forced to face karmic numbers. Only those who have abused the natural laws in past lives, and now must pay the price, are affected.

Karmic numbers fourteen, sixteen, nineteen, and sometimes thirteen are often considered malific (malicious) in effect, but actually they are reconstructive, for they have lessons to teach which can lead you to gain necessary experience. They warn you to adjust your life so that the weakness does not cause you continued heartaches.

YOU MUST PAY THE KARMIC DEBT

While any reconstruction period seems like a calamity while transiting its vibrations, the tests or trials experienced are actually good for you. One of the cosmic laws states that you must pay for transgressions you have committed either in this life or a former incarnation. On the other hand, you will also reap the reward of any good deeds. If you understand the warnings and seek to balance the account of your misdeeds by paying the debt, then you'll gradually cancel the unfortunate effect.

WHAT THE KARMIC NUMBERS ARE

The karmic numbers are 13, 14, 16, and 19. They may occur as the total of your soul's urge, destiny, birthpath, or power numbers. An explanation of them follows.

MALIFIC OR KARMIC NUMBER THIRTEEN

(13)

The Tarot card for arcanum thirteen is entitled "Death" or "The Reaper." It is symbolized by the skeleton, which is the accepted figure for death, taken figuratively. You fear death mainly because you fear the unknown beyond the grave. The actual interpretation is that death does not mean the end of life, but it constitutes change, motion, or transformation. Change is what we call death. In other words, death is a rebirth, renewal, and an inspirational beginning. The thirteenth card or karmic number signifies that death is merely a change of consciousness.

Through superstition the number thirteen came into ill repute. It really is a period of regeneration. The keyword is work on the material plane. The warning given is that there is danger of backsliding into laziness, negativity, and inefficiency. Trials and tests of proficiency will be given on the material plane, and work is the solution. It warns against being indifferent, discontented, and ill-mannered.

MALIFIC OR KARMIC NUMBER FOURTEEN

(14)

Arcanum *fourteen* represents physical possessions. It warns of loss of property and failure in business. It is hard for a *fourteen* to learn his lesson, because he often tries to gain freedom by destructive methods or at the expense of others. This brings loss, sickness and death. You are too interested in physical senses. *Fourteen* has also been called the number of experience.

If *fourteen* is found as the total vowel number, then you'll experience many emotional upsets and delays.

If *fourteen* occurs as the total destiny number, many disappointments and losses will be encountered.

If *fourteen* is the total of the birthpath, you must learn the lesson of detachment. This means to have and let go.

The basic message of the warning number *fourteen* is lack of understanding. Often we don't understand the motives of others, not even our own, for we act one way and think and feel in another. Through understanding we develop humility, compassion, and overflowing love. We should avoid going to extremes. Be temperate.

MALIFIC OR KARMIC NUMBER SIXTEEN

(16)

Tarot card number *sixteen* entitled "The Tower" depicts ruin. The falling tower indicates the crushing of human pride and vanity. The structure was built of ignorance and wrong doing, through self-will and a self-centered life. Not until we understand the true nature of willpower do we destroy false ideas, and learn what is right.

Number *sixteen* warns of some strange calamity, defeat of plans, disgrace, accidents, deception, and adversity. It indicates the karma of former illegitimate love affairs. Number *sixteen* offers the test of optimism and faith.

If number *sixteen* is found as the total of the soul's urge, it shows false friends and broken dreams. If it appears as the destiny number, it warns of loss of name, position, fortune, and power. If it is the number of the total birthpath, then all tragedies must be learned—love to lose, rise to fall. You must not cling to the material.

KARMIC NUMBER NINETEEN

(19)

Tarot card number *nineteen* symbolizes the "Sun" or "Reunion." It is not inanimate, but a living force.

Nineteen is the equalizer, or collector. It demands an "eye for an eye." We get out of life just what we put into it.

Number *nineteen* warns you not to be domineering, but exercise tolerance. You formerly took something, and now you must pay it back. It is a test of endurance.

If your soul's urge totals *nineteen*, then you'll have to face all of life's secrets which may have been hidden and are now dragged out.

If *nineteen* occurs as a total of your destiny, you may find you have lost everything at the end of your life.

If *nineteen* occurs as the total number of your birthpath, then you must meet your failings, and reap what you have sown. Even though you'd like to be free, you must now pay the piper.

If *nineteen* occurs as the total of either your heart or destiny number, it means you brought this karma over from a previous life. It is a weakness in character which must be overcome by living up to the digits of the test number.

WHAT YOU SHOULD DO
WITH YOUR KARMIC NUMBERS

If you have one or more of these malific or karmic numbers as a total in any of the places mentioned, then read what you should do to pay your karmic debt. If you do not have any of the karmic numbers, then your account on earth is balanced, and you are free, with no Karmic obligations to bar your success. Now set up your own name to determine if you are free of any karmic debt. Remember, the karmic numbers are 13, 14, 16, 19.

SEVENTEEN

The Significance of the First Vowel in Your First Name

If you want to be the center of attention at a party, are uncertain how to proceed to win the friendship of a specific individual, or are in a quandary or in doubt as to how to handle children, then take numerological notice of the first vowel in his first name, or the nickname by which he is known. The *first vowel* shows his emotional impulse, his attitude, and how he will respond or react, namely, how he will predictably think and act.

WHAT THE FIRST VOWELS ARE

The single vowels are A, E, I, O, U, *and* Y, when there is no other vowel in the syllable. "W" if used as a vowel cannot stand alone as the first letter of a name. It always follows another vowel, such as in EWELL, and is an undeveloped vowel. Therefore, unlike some numerologists, I do not use it as a vowel, for it is dual, unstable, and vacillating, and cannot function alone. However, I will give you its interpretation should you decide to treat it as a vowel.

Vowels are of three types: Long, short, and diphthong as described below. If a vowel is long, the attributes are strongly pronounced. If it is short, it is less dynamic in expression. If the vowel occurs in a diphthong it is dual in nature, and its strength is divided with the other vowel, the two vowels being expressed together.

The first vowel of your first name shows your reaction to outer stimuli, or how you will think, act, and behave.

156

Examples of Long Vowels Are:

A as in Amy; *E* and in Edith; *I* as in Ivan; *O* and in Joseph; *U* as in Judith; *Y* as in Byron; *W*–none.

Examples of Short Vowels Are:

A as in Cameron; *E* as in Nedson; *I* as in Virginia; *O* as in Ronald; *U* as in Duncan; *Y* as in Lydia; *W*–none.

Examples of Diphthong Vowels Are:

A as in Pauline; *E* as in Eunice; *I* as in Diana; *O* as in Joan; *U* as in Duane; *Y* as in Joyce; *W* as in Jewel.

WHAT YOUR FIRST VOWELS TELL YOU

Vowel "A"

The vowel "A," with a numerical value of *one*, is mental in aspect, but it is also emotional, for it has considerable feeling. As a first vowel it is progressive, adventurous, independent, and original. Having a pioneering spirit, it will push ahead. If *A* is the first vowel of your first name, you will be interested in new ideas, but you will prefer that they come from your fertile mind rather than from another, for you like to be creative. You enjoy being different. You will defend your own viewpoint even though the whole world opposes you. Since you refuse to be driven, you will accept advice only when it coincides with what you already believe, and then merely to double check your own views.

A invites new contacts, new opportunities, and new activities involving change. You want to break away from old or tried traditions and venture into the unknown.

If your first vowel is *A*, you must guard against being domineering, opinionated, and having false pride. You should learn to be tolerant, yet never lose your individuality.

Vowel "E"

The vowel "E" with the numerical value of *five*, is physical in aspect, and is related to the five senses. It has been labelled the spice of life, for it likes variety, change, and action.

If your first vowel is *E*, you want freedom above everything for growth, but you should not break rules to get it. *E* is called the number of experience, and it occurs in names more often than any other vowel or letter. Under *E* the unexpected is the rule. Many problems arise because of hasty action. If *E* is your first vowel, public contact will bring enjoyment and often travel. Money has a way of being plentiful one minute and scarce the next, because of the "easy-come-easy-go" attitude of an *E*.

Marriage partnerships may be unstable, and the home may suffer due to the fluctuating worldly living and impulsive actions. Life's experiences, which will be many, are enacted as on a stage or in a glass house. You will experience many exciting conditions, opportunities, and problems. Therefore, you should keep up-to-date, for you may meet the unexpected momentarily. You must learn to overcome temptation and excessive indulgences, especially in regard to the opposite sex. You must guard against being too restless and changeable, especially in matters of love and speculation.

Vowel "I"

The vowel "I," which has the numerical value of *nine*, must cultivate universal love and understanding. If the first vowel of your first name is *I*, you are intense, emotional, and have a abundance of vital energy. You are a law unto yourself. If you have many *I*'s in your name, you will be sensitive to the point of being touchy, but you will be sympathetic.It may bring delays, for it is dual and a repeater. It is either the genius or the bum, the spreader of illumination or of terror. It is either quiet, energetic, and helpful, or erratic and selfish. An *I* is often bored or indifferent even though he has many talents. He does not like change, for he does not like to try anything new. He prefers to perfect what he knows, and then stick to the tried method, repeating it constantly. Heart and passion rule the mind of *I*. If he is well developed, he is sympathetic, and loves to serve humanity; if not, he is self-centered, and self-indulgent.

The vowel *I* can attract wealth and protection. He has the ability to understand the needs of others and so can pave the way for success and a fortune. If *I* is a failure, it is due to too much optimism, causing him to make mistakes.

If his intuitive sense is developed, he has creative talent.

He must guard against being moody, for this may lead to loss of opportunity.

Vowel "O"

The vowel "O," with a numerical value of *six*, is happiest when giving advice to others, or when counseling them. *O* likes to be useful, and is essentially the teacher or parent.

If your first vowel is *O*, you need responsibility in order to feel important. You want a chance to shine in the home ar l community. You should avoid arguing. Even though you enjoy trying to convince others that you are right, you often arouse antagonism. If you must argue, be sure to be tactful.

Since you are an excellent host and a good cook, people look forward to an invitation to a party at your home. You are interested in improvements.

The interest of *O* runs to old established businesses. This gives him the opportunity or the desire to settle down in one place and not be forced to move. *O* needs harmony and beauty in his surroundings, and he enjoys working in a garden.

The first vowel *O* gives the opportunity to serve the community. He is often bound to the traditional.

Many constructive *O's* have a talent for music, the arts, and poetry.

Too many *O's* might indicate stubbornness, slowness, and despondency.

Vowel "U"

If the first vowel of your first name is "U," your approach is essentially that of a carefree, jovial, and happy person. Since you are outstanding in repartee, you could qualify as an after dinner speaker, for you have the gift of using words effectively. You are liked by most people, and are a good friend in return. You may attract peculiar experiences, suffering because of them. You are a nature lover, and make flowers and plants grow profusely. You are a good judge of perfumes and antiques.

Some *U's* are fond of study and mental analysis. Names with *U* as the first vowel are emotional. They may express themselves in several lines. They are artistic, and often engage in a profession. They must direct their efforts with an iron willpower to fight their excessive emotional quality. Often they succumb to unconventional love affairs.

U wants to branch out and do something different. The success of a *U* will come through creative activity. Self-improvement is their keynote.

They are usually charming and popular in groups, for they extend love and friendship to others. *U* is conservative and does not seek the initiative. He should rely on his intuition. A developed *U* will strive to uplift mankind. If living negatively, he will be selfish and narrow-minded.

Vowel "Y"

The first vowel "Y," with a value of *seven,* can be used either as a vowel or consonant. If there is no other vowel in the syllable, then *Y* will always be a vowel. It is more inclined to lean than be dominant or independent. Although it needs protection, it is able to draw a cloak around itself.

Y is introspective. Being strongly intuitive, it should follow its hunches. *Y's* force is intellectual and logical. *Y* is closely alligned with nature, but it has difficulty expressing itself freely.

If the first vowel of your first name is *Y,* you can gain much by being tactful and diplomatic, knowing when to speak, and when to keep quiet. You love to penetrate into the depths to gain knowledge and psychic phenomena.

A *Y* is worth cultivating. With your secretive disposition, you keep many things to yourself, refusing to share your secrets with even your closest friend or relative. You like to spend some time alone in quietude and reflection. A *Y* is difficult to understand, for he bottles up his feelings. He admires intellectual pursuits, and mental courage.

You must learn to be discriminating. Otherwise, you may be deceived by appearancees. A *Y* becomes developed through silent study, prayer, observation, and meditation. If living negatively, you lack tact, analysis, and knowledge.

Vowel "EW"

The letter "W" is never used alone as a first letter vowel. It occurs only in combination with another vowel, and each gets equal recognition. The EW is composed of two fives, namely, *E* equals 5, and *W* equals five or a ten, giving it the value of *A* or 1, to a certain degree. Being made up of two fives, EW depends on the opposite sex to accomplish its purpose in life.

When *W* is used as a combination vowel, it is dual in nature, and can be a force for good or bad. It is a follower and not a leader.

HOW YOU CAN ENTERTAIN GUESTS AT A PARTY
BY PLAYING THE GAME OF VOWELS

Do you want to be the life of the party at your home or even in a church circle? You can be in great demand, and the most popular person present, simply by applying the information gained concerning first vowels. This is the manner in which you can do it:

> Take a pencil and pad (or you can do it orally with no props) and go around the group asking each person his first name or the nickname by which he is called. Then quickly analyze the individual by using the first vowel of his first name as your clue. Be sure you have studied each vowel thoroughly so that you are accurate in your interpretation.

EIGHTEEN

How to Use Numerology to Predict the Future

Since my primary purpose in writing this self-help book of numerology is to teach you to help yourself, thus getting the most out of your life by learning to interpret the hidden meaning behind the numbers, I have included this valuable information on predictions in this book. To my knowledge no one has ever presented this scientific system of predictions to the public. It represents over twenty-five years of experience and hard work on my part, gained through observation, trial and error, and research.

NO GUESS WORK OR LUCK INVOLVED
IN NUMEROLOGY FORETELLING THE FUTURE

My system of foretelling the future is based on the esoteric meaning behind numbers, and not on speculation. There is no element of good or bad luck involved, for my calculations are derived from your entire birthpath which, like nature, is immutable and unchangeable. The key to these predictions is found in the ancient Tarot pack of cards. By studying diligently and digging into numerology you can discern the propitious time for you to begin a new undertaking, the wisdom of delay and inaction at certain periods in order to avoid loss or disappointments, and the time to guard your health and finances.

Every cycle in your life, and each is numbered, follows a definite order. Nothing in the world happens by accident. There's a correct time to begin every new venture, and a favorable time to have patience and lie low. Your individual year is figured from one birthday to the next, and not according to the calendar year.

162

Example:

If your birthday is in May, your year will extend from May to May, and not from January to January as the calendar portrays. Your birthpath is divided into three sections, namely, month, day, and year plus your key to character. The first cycle governs the overtone for the entire year. The next three four month cycles are figured and then balanced with the overtone. The last includes the key to character arrived at through figuring the system of the Magi.

HOW TO CONSULT THE TABLE TO
HELP YOU FIND THE KEY

Notice: In order to help you determine your predictions more readily, and also to relieve you of detailed computation, I have already figured for you the key to character for every day in the calendar year. All you need now do is to turn to the table to copy the key to character, and use it instead of tediously figuring the system of the magi. However, for those who are scientifically inclined and want to know how I arrived at my conclusion (key), I have given you the exact process step for step.

SYSTEM OF THE MAGI:
HOW TO FIND YOUR KEY TO CHARACTER

Example:

Your date of birth is December 11th.

If your birthday is on December eleventh of any year, consult the table for the value of the month of December, (31). Subtract your birthday (11) from this. This gives your path in life, namely (31-11 equals 20). Add the path together to get the problem (2 plus 0 equals 2). From the path subtract 13-26-39-52, the highest number possible in order to leave a remainder. This is the Method number or the Magi, namely, 20-13 equals 7. From the Magi subtract the problem, or the problem from the Magi, whichever is the larger (7-2 equals 5). To this remainder (5) add the degree of birth (see table) thus, 5 plus 21 degrees equals 26. Reduce this to a single digit to get the key to character (2 plus 6 equals 8). The key to character is eight. To check this turn to

December 11th in the table. Notice, it has already been figured for you as eight. Following is another example for you to work out and check results. Let's assume your date of birth is:

February 27th

Consult the table for the value of February. It is fifty-one (51).

February 51

Subtract birthday . . . . . . <u>27</u>

Path 24

Add path for problem . . . <u>6</u>   (2 plus 4 equals 6)

Subt. 13 from path 11   (24 – 13 equals 11)
                                        Method of Magi
Subt. probl. from Magi . .   5   (11 – 6 equals 5)

Add degree of birth 14   (5 plus 9 equals 14)
                                        9 equals degrees
Reduce to single digit . . . 5   (1 plus 4 equals 5).
                                        Key to char.

However, all you need do is to consult the table already figured for you to obtain your key to character.

STEP-UP–PROCESS

When after subtracting the birthdate from the number of the month, the remainder is too small to allow subtraction of thirteen, use the step-up process taking the birthdate for the path. Add the birthdate to get the problem. The remainder after subtracting the birthdate from the number of the month is called the Method of the Magi. Proceed as usual.

TABLE OF SYSTEM OF MAGI

January	53	March	49
February	51	April	47

May 45   September 37

June 43   October 35

July 41   November 33

August 39   December 31

SUITS:

Hearts 13   equals spring, love, friends

Clubs 26   equals summer, knowledge, news

Diamonds 39   equals autumn, wealth, money

Spades 52   equals winter, business, labor

You need not figure the STEP-UP PROCESS. It is already included in arriving at the KEY.

TABLE OF THE DEGREE OF THE DAY OF BIRTH IN EACH SIGN OF THE ZODIAC

Date of Birth		Degree	Key	Date of Birth		Degree	Key
January	1	12	9	January	16	27	10
	2	13	8		17	28	11
	3	14	2		18	29	3
	4	15	9		19	30	4
	5	16	10		20	1	2
	6	17	2		21	2	3
	7	18	3		22	3	4
	8	19	4		23	4	5
	9	20	5		24	5	13
	10	21	6		25	6	5
	11	22	7		26	7	6
	12	23	8		27	8	4
	13	24	9		28	9	5
	14	25	8		29	10	6
	15	26	9		30	11	7
					31	12	8

Date of Birth	Degree	Key	Date of Birth	Degree	Key
February 1	13	10	February 16	28	11
2	14	8	17	29	3
3	15	9	18	30	4
4	16	10	19	1	2
5	17	2	20	2	3
6	18	3	21	3	4
7	19	4	22	4	1
8	20	5	23	5	4
9	21	6	24	6	5
10	22	7	25	7	12
11	23	8	26	8	4
12	24	7	27	9	5
13	25	8	28	10	6
14	26	9	29	11	7
15	27	10			
March 1	11	5	March 16	26	9
2	12	6	17	27	10
3	13	7	18	28	11
4	14	8	19	29	3
5	15	9	20	30	11
6	16	10	21	1	9
7	17	2	22	2	10
8	18	3	23	3	8
9	19	4	24	4	9
10	20	3	25	5	10
11	21	4	26	6	2
12	22	5	27	7	3
13	23	6	28	8	4
14	24	7	29	9	5
15	25	8	30	10	5
			31	11	6
April 1	12	6	April 9	20	3
2	13	7	10	21	4
3	14	8	11	22	5
4	15	9	12	23	6
5	16	10	13	24	7
6	17	2	14	25	8
7	18	3	15	26	9
8	19	2	16	27	10

Date of Birth Degree Key   *Date of Birth Degree Key*

April	17	28	11	April	24	5	10
	18	29	10		25	6	11
	19	30	11		26	7	3
	20	1	9		27	8	4
	21	2	7		28	9	4
	22	3	8		29	10	5
	23	4	9		30	11	6

May	1	12	6	May	16	27	8
	2	13	7		17	28	9
	3	14	8		18	29	10
	4	15	9		19	30	8
	5	16	10		20	1	6
	6	17	9		21	2	7
	7	18	1		22	3	8
	8	19	2		23	4	9
	9	20	3		24	5	1
	10	21	4		25	6	11
	11	22	5		26	7	11
	12	23	6		27	8	3
	13	24	7		28	9	4
	14	25	8		29	10	5
	15	26	9		30	11	6
					31	12	7

June	1	13	7	June	16	28	9
	2	14	8		17	29	7
	3	15	9		18	30	8
	4	16	8		19	1	6
	5	17	9		20	2	6
	6	18	10		21	3	7
	7	19	2		22	2	7
	8	20	3		23	3	8
	9	21	4		24	3	7
	10	22	5		25	4	8
	11	23	6		26	4	8
	12	24	7		27	5	9
	13	25	8		28	5	9
	14	26	7		29	6	1
	15	27	8		30	7	8

Date of Birth	Degree	Key	Date of Birth		
July 1	8	11	July 16	23	10
2	9	1	17	24	11
3	10	11	18	25	3
4	11	3	19	26	4
5	12	4	20	27	5
6	13	5	21	28	6
7	14	6	22	29	6
8	15	7	23	30	7
9	16	8	24	1	5
10	17	9	25	2	6
11	18	10	26	3	7
12	19	9	27	4	8
13	20	10	28	5	8
14	21	11	29	6	7
15	22	9	30	7	6
			31	8	5
August 1	9	10	August 16	24	11
2	10	11	17	25	3
3	11	3	18	26	4
4	12	4	19	27	5
5	13	5	20	28	5
6	14	6	21	29	6
7	15	7	22	30	7
8	16	8	23	1	5
9	17	9	24	2	6
10	18	8	25	3	7
11	19	9	26	4	9
12	20	10	27	5	8
13	21	8	28	6	7
14	22	9	29	7	8
15	23	10	30	8	5
			31	9	4
September 1	10	11	September 6	15	7
2	11	3	7	16	8
3	12	4	8	17	7
4	13	5	9	18	8
5	14	6	10	19	9

Date of Birth	Degree	Key	Date of Birth	Degree	Key
September 11	20	7	September 21	30	7
12	21	8	22	1	5
13	22	9	23	2	6
14	23	10	24	3	1
15	24	11	25	4	9
16	25	3	26	5	8
17	26	4	27	6	7
18	27	4	28	7	8
19	28	5	29	8	11
20	29	6	30	9	4
October 1	10	11	October 16	25	11
2	11	3	17	26	3
3	12	4	18	27	4
4	13	5	19	28	5
5	14	6	20	29	6
6	15	5	21	30	7
7	16	6	22	1	1
8	17	7	23	2	9
9	18	5	24	3	8
10	19	6	25	4	7
11	20	7	26	5	6
12	21	8	27	6	7
13	22	9	28	7	1
14	23	10	29	8	4
15	24	11	30	9	11
			31	10	1
November 1	11	3	November 14	24	10
2	12	4	15	25	11
3	13	5	16	26	3
4	14	4	17	27	4
5	15	5	18	28	5
6	16	6	19	29	6
7	17	4	20	30	5
8	18	5	21	1	1
9	19	6	22	2	9
10	20	7	23	3	8
11	21	8	24	4	7
12	22	9	25	5	6
13	23	10	26	6	7

Date of Birth	Degree	Key	Date of Birth	Degree	Key
November 27	7	1	November 29	9	7
28	8	4	30	10	1
December 1	11	3	December 16	26	3
2	12	2	17	27	4
3	13	3	18	28	5
4	14	4	19	29	4
5	15	2	20	30	12
6	16	3	21	1	8
7	17	4	22	2	7
8	18	5	23	3	6
9	19	6	24	4	5
10	20	7	25	5	6
11	21	8	26	6	9
12	22	8	27	7	3
13	23	9	28	8	6
14	24	10	29	9	9
15	25	11	30	10	3
			31	11	4

MEANING OF YOUR KEY TO CHARACTER

Number 1. Are dominant and headstrong, usually insisting on ruling.

Number 2. Are doormats, peacemakers, diplomats, and martyrs to family.

Number 3. Find it hard to make decisions. See too many sides to an issue.

Number 4. Seek to be satisfied with existing conditions which kills ambition.

Number 5. Restless people needing change. Often sex is strong. Travel much.

Number 6. Stubborn and argumentative, set. Interested in civic affairs and home.

Number 7. Tragic key. Struggles and obstacles, but psychic perception.

Number 8. Power to draw what needs. Financial security in old age.

Number 9. Disappointments, unhappy love affairs, frustration, religious leader.

Number 10. Success, dominance, leadership, and a pioneering spirit.

Number 11. Inspirational and spiritual. Negative traveler. Often vacillating.

Number 12. Feminine power to sway. Get own way thru arousing Sympathy and tact.

Number 13. Positive dominant force. Can't be ruled or managed. Take what you want.

MEANING OF YOUR FOUR MONTHS' CYCLES—PREDICTIONS

Foretelling Your Future

Number 13. A warning number. Indicates change of plans or place. Is the number of death, but if lived through is like a rebirth or new start. Does not occur often.

Number 14. Good for dealing with money, speculation, or changes in business, but some risk is involved. Sometimes indicates unwise divorce. Is monotonous and plodding period. Usually working out of social and family obligations.

Number 15. Is the personal number. Brings love, joy, and sorrow. Indicates births, love affairs, and in combination with 18, death or divorce. Good for getting money or favors from others.

Number 16. The unexpected. Symbolizes accidents, trouble, but sometime brings unexpected opportunities. Not a good time to take a trip or sign papers without seeking expert advice.

Number 17. Good financial vibration. Use knowledge gained from past experiences to deal with present situation. Star of hope or Magi, which means it is a fortunate number.

Number 18. Indicates calamity, quarrels, wars, revolutions, and enemies. Worst vibration possible. Papers should be signed carefully or not at all. Must guard against deception in business and personal affairs. No time to travel or start anything new.

Number 19. Fortunate number. Promises success, happiness, and honor. Nineteen is a connubial number. While 15 applies to one person, 19, a love vibration, applies to two. A peaceful vibration.

Number 20. A good change but not necessarily of location or environment. One of the best numbers . . . new activities, interests, and a happy busy period. Good for planning for next year. Many old people die during this number. Seventeen, twenty-one, and twenty are the best vibrations.

Number 21. Period of assured success. A time to carry out plans, take journeys, and make investments. It's fortunate for future events. You can accomplish what you desire under a twenty-one.

Number 22. It is best not to act, but if you do, be sure to consult someone who is well informed. Be careful. Time for false judgment. May be time of many decisions or one. Can't trust own judgment. Affairs will be in a pivotal state and about to break.

Number 23. Brings many changes, sometimes legal proceedings and settling of estates. Often extensive traveling. Peculiar vibration, with nervous and high tension. Often needs a doctor. New contacts. Middle-aged women who let twenty-three rule are in danger of losing their minds. It can mean success.

Number 24. Family love vibration. Always a family affair. May bring illness in the home. Gain through love and the opposite sex. Favorable for future plans.

Number 25. Path of trial, petty annoyances, annoying health conditions. Sometimes brings illness or death of elderly people.

Number 26. Splendid financial number, but if good judgment is not used, can throw away all you've accumulated. Many people die of a stroke in a twenty-six period. Watch partnerships, investments, and bad speculation. Warning to be careful.

Number 27. Same as 18. Period of troubles and calamities. Not a favorable time to start anything.

Notice: Numbers usually do not go beyond these, but if you encounter any, the following synopsis tells what they can mean.

Number 28. Contradictions, Loss through trust in others, opposition and competition. Can be either fortunate of unfortunate.

Number 29. Unexpected danger. Warning for future. Uncertainties, deception, treachery.

Number 30. Neither fortunate nor unfortunate. Thoughtful deduction, retrospection, and mental superiority over others. Can be powerful.

Number 31. Much like thirty except even more self-contained, lonely, and isolated from friends. Not fortunate from worldly standpoint. Wavering.

Number 32. Magical power like five, fourteen, or twenty-three. For tunate if held to own judgment. Favorable for future.

Number 33. Same meaning as 24 or 15.

Number 34. Same as 25.

Number 35. Same as 17 or 26.

Number 36. Same as 27.

Number 37. Good and fortunate in friendships, love, partnerships.

Number 38. Same as 29.

Number 39. Same as 30.

Number 40. Same as 31.

Number 41. Same as 32.

Number 42. Same as 33.

Number 43. Unfortunate number. Revolution, failure, not good.

Number 44. Same as 26.
Number 45. Same as 27.
Number 46. Same as 37.
Number 47. Same as 29.
Number 48. Same as 30.
Number 49. Same as 13 or 22.

The following is the meaning of combinations of numbers. It refers to the overtone plus one of the periods in question. As you continue to work with figures, new combinations will prove themselves to be right. Thus you will be able to interpret them.

COMBINATION OF NUMBERS—
OVERTONE WITH ONE OF THE PERIODS

15-18 When a fifteen is followed by an 18, it usually means divorce or separation or both. Suggests personal calamity.

15-20 Change for the better in personal matters—work, home, travel, health.

15-22 Personal decision. Don't trust own judgment. Much restlessness.

15-23 Guard health. You sense change and so are restless and apprehensive.

15-16 Unexpected personal matters—accidents, danger of fall.

15-17 Personal key to happiness.

15-19 Love vibration.

15-21 Violent death, or end of some phase.

15-24 Great joy or sorrow.

16-16 Short journeys. Be very careful.

16-17 Unexpected increase in income, or return to value of holdings. Good time to sell real estate, but with no long listings.

16-18 Reconstruction period. Usually this is a disastrous combination Indicates danger from accidents, divorce, enemies.

16-20 Always a good change, or an unexpected opportunity.

16-21 Good for work or carrying out plans. Guard against accidents.

16-23 Apt to produce unwise divorce or breed love affairs. May bring a new business opportunity or trip.

17-18 Financial difficulties.

17-19 Good money year. Good for planning for following year. May show tendency to brood which might lead to suicide.

17-20 Return to value of investments that have lain dormant.

17-22 Indicates business decision.

17, 20, and 21 are the best vibrations.

18, 22, and 14 indicate that the harder one works the less he accomplishes.

18-14 Adverse period.

18-15 Not good.

18-18 Be careful. Plan.

18-24 Menace of illness that could be disastrous. Sometimes beginning of divorce proceedings.

18-16 Indicates a reconstruction period. It's usually good, for the old foundation was not firm. Seems like a calamity while in it.

19-15 Love strongly indicated.

19-19 Don't put name to anything not necessary.

19-21 In aged often brings completion.

19-22 Personal matter decision to be made. It often concerns marriage.

19-23 Beginning of good years. Strange change of some sort and often legal affairs.

20-18 Hesitate to make change—might be unsatisfactory or temporary.

20-16 Always good change or unexpected opportunity.

20-19 Marriage year. Travel and change of location through marriage. Increase in earnings or better position.

20-14 Change would bring hard work but would be good.

20-21 Assured success in a new venture. Excellent for travel or carrying out plans.

20-24 Family affairs. Change for better. Finances good. Remodeling or change in home.

20-23 Change of location to strange place. Travel or change of home.

21-19 Could be proposal, engagement, or marriage. If married may bring pregnancy or birth of child. Good time to purchase home.

21-23 Legal matters, health, travel, and new interests.

21-24 Home and family matters assured success.

22-22 Be cautious, especially in making decisions.

22-21 Time to make wise decisions and put plans into effect.

22-23 Decision concerning legal matters, travel, health. Unwise love affairs.

22-24 Decision concerning family matters, children, surgery, housing of old.

23-17 Year to guard health. Change for good in finances. Guard against surgery.

HOW TO WORK OUT PREDICTIONS

Your year does not coincide with the present year until after your birthday in all calculations. In other words, if you are now twenty-one years old, and you are figuring your chart in March 1971, but your birthday is not until July 1971, you must use the age of twenty-one and the year of 1970 in your calculations. If you are figuring the chart after July, you should use the age of twenty-two and the year of 1971. I'll explain this in another way. The year 1970 would be considered the present year for you until your birthday in July, even though the calendar indicates the date as March, 1971.

The following steps will help you to figure your predictions:

Step 1. To find the overtone for the total year, add the sum of the year of your birth to the present year and reduce.

Step 2. For the first four months' period, add your present age to the present year and reduce.

Step 3. For the second four months, add your total birthpath to the present year and reduce.

Step 4. For the third and last four months, add the key to character (see table) to the present year and reduce.

Now we'll set up a birthdate so that you will know how to figure the predictions.

Example: Your Birthday is on February 27, 1946.

February	27	1946
2	9	20 equals 13, equals 4

You are figuring the chart on March 1, 1972. Proceed as follows:

OVERTONE	First period	Second period	Third period
For year	(Feb. 27-June 27)	(June 27-Oct. 27)	(Oct. 27-Feb. 27)
1972	1972	1972	1972
20	26	13	7
1992 (21)	1998 (27)	1985 (23)	1979 (26)

Overtone (21); First period (27); Second period (23); Third Period (26).

The overtone for the entire year, from February 27, 1972 to February 27, 1973, is twenty-one. It is found by adding the year of birth (1946 equals 20) to the present year (1972), and reducing this to twenty-one (1 plus 9 plus 9 plus 2 equals 21). The twenty-one overtone is the best number possible. It indicates a good time to carry out plans, take trips, and make investments. It has an overall successful aspect. However, you must also look at the subperiods into which the year is divided. From February 27 to June 27, the prevailing number is twenty-seven. This is found by adding the present age of twenty-six to the present year (1972). You arrive at your age by subtracting your year of birth (1946) from the present year (1972). The result is twenty-seven, which augurs delays and adverse conditions even with the twenty-one overtone. It is equal to an eighteen, which while seemingly unproductive, is actually a reconstruction period paving the way for better future events.

Following this the second four months' period is governed by the number twenty-three. This period runs from June 27 to October 27th. It is found by adding the birthpath (2 plus 9 plus 20 equals thirteen) to the present year 1972. This equals 1985, which is twenty-three reduced. With the overtone of twenty-one, the twenty-three (21-23) indicates legal matters, health, travel, and new interests. Twenty-three is a peculiar vibration and requires a powerful protector, which is usually a doctor. It can be a nervous and restless period. It may also bring new contacts, and travel to distant parts. The last period from October 27th to February 27th, winding up the year or third period, is governed by the number twenty-six. It is found by adding the key to character (7) (see table) to the present year of 1972. Thus 1972 equals 19 plus 7 equals 26. Twenty-six can be an excellent vibration, but unless good judgment is used, you can throw away or lose a fortune. With the twenty-one overtone, it should be a good money making period, but investments and partnerships should be watched. Some people die of a stroke in a twenty-six period.

Now we'll figure another chart with a different aspect.

Example: Let's Figure Your Birthday is:

AUGUST   6   1946

6   6   20 = 16

You are figuring the chart in March 1971. You must use the year 1970 for your calculations until after your birthday in

August, 1971. If you were figuring the chart in September 1971 (after your birthday) then you would use the present year of 1971. Proceed as follows:

OVERTONE	First period	Second period	Third period
for year	(Aug. 6-Dec. 6)	(Dec. 6-Apr. 6)	(Apr. 6-Aug. 6)
1970	1070	1970	1970
20	24	16	6 (key)
1990 = 19	1994 = 23	1986 = 24	1976 = 23

Overtone (19); First period (23); Second period (24); Third period (23).

The overtone of nineteen for the entire year from August 6, 1970 to August 6, 1971 is a fortunate number. With the 23 of the first period from August 6th to December 6th (19-23) it suggests the beginning of good years with some strange change taking place. This could involve legal affairs. While fifteen applies to one person only, nineteen usually means two or more individuals and is often a love vibration. The twenty-three is a peculiar vibration and often suggests an illness, but with the nineteen overtone it can mean new contacts during the four months' period. It usually is a nervous period. The second four months' period runs from December 6, 1970 to April 6, 1971. The ruling vibration is twenty-four. The twenty-four is centered around the home, and concerns family matters. This can mean the care and responsibility of children or old people. With the nineteen overtone (19-24) it is a good period, governed by love. It means home and family matters will be successful. It may bring illness, but this will not be of a serious nature. The last or third period runs from April 6, 1971 to August 6, 1971 with a ruling vibration of twenty-three. This is the same vibration as that of the second period and carries the same interpretation. With a key to character of six, you must try to avoid arguments, for you could be obstinate and opinionated.

Now are you beginning to get the feel of figuring predictions? I'll give you another example. See if you can figure this alone, and then check with my interpretation.

Sugar Ray Robinson, the prize-fighter, has a given name at birth of Walker Smith. He was born on May 3, 1921. You are figuring the chart in March 1972. Since it is such a short time until his birthday, you may wish to only set up the third or last period running from January 3 to May 3, 1971. He has not as yet had a birthday in 1972.

May   3   1921

5   3   13   = (5 + 3 + 4 = 12 = 3)

All you need do is set up the overtone and the last period with the key, because he is now in the last period.

Thus:

1971		1971	
13		8	(key)
1984	= 22	1979	= 26

The last period before his birthday (which runs from January to May) is the 22-26 combination. The overtone augurs uncertainty, and a time to watch himself for he could make the wrong decision. His own judgment is not to be trusted in a twenty-two. He should consult someone in better numbers for advice. With the twenty-six (22-26) it means he must be very careful lest he lose everything.

Now we'll proceed to figure the year 1972. Actually, I usually. set up the whole year instead of the fragments given above even though the predictions are past, for it gives me a better perspective of the past year and the present one to get the feel of prevailing conditions.

We'll now set up his predictions for 1972.

OVERTONE for year	First period (May 3-Sept. 3)	Second period (Sept. 3-Jan. 3)	Third period (Jan. 3-May 3
1972	1972	1972	1972
13	51	12	8 (key)
1985 = 23	2023 = 25	1984 = 22	19801 = 18

Overtone (23); First period (25); Second period (22); Third period (18).

With an eight key to character, Sugar Ray Robinson need never know actual want, for he can always find a way out of a bad situation. It is an excellent key to help him make money.

The overtone of twenty-three for the year 1972 is a tricky one. It can mean changes and travel, but it usually means a decision must be made. With the twenty-five vibration of the first period from May 3 to September 3, the (23-25) combination is not good, for it can mean that his trials and difficulties will be physical and medical attention will be required. It is a time to watch his health.

The second period running from September 1972 to January 3, 1973 is governed by the number twenty-two. With the overtone of 23, making (23-22) it suggests decisions must be made concerning legal matters or health. Twenty-two is a time to move slowly and carefully, for he is not under good vibrations to trust his own judgment.

The last period from January 3rd to May 3rd has an eighteen vibration. This again is not a good period, for eighteen suggests to be very careful for fear of disaster. With the twenty-three overtone (23-18) it means menace of an illness that could be very troublesome. Sometimes this combination suggests divorce proceedings.

Being able to foretell your future and that of others is not a matter of fortune-telling. It is based on actual figures. Therefore, if you follow the dictates of the numbers given, your predictions should not vary, even though you may have a lapse of months between figuring your numeroscope.

NINETEEN

How to Select Partners in Marriage, Business, and for Social Purposes

One reason for the prevalence of divorces these days is that one frequently chooses one's opposite in marriage. One is often attracted to a person who thinks and acts differently than you do, for the reason that he or she possesses the qualities which you lack. This selection of a mate does not often engender lasting ties, or produce marital bliss, for the marriage partners will fail to have a mutual understanding.

HOW TO SELECT YOUR PARTNER
IN MARRIAGE

It's time you changed your viewpoint if you expect to have a lasting union in marriage. You should select a marriage partner based on the law of similars and not on extremes or opposites in marriage. The more similar vibrations you have, the better chance you have of continued harmony in the marriage union. It is still customary for a woman to change her name in marriage to conform to her husband's surname. This will insure the couple at least one point in harmony.

WHOM YOU SHOULD MARRY

If you are planning on getting married, instead of relying solely on the pinnacles and the personal year, which are very important but which will change eventually, it would be more expedient for you to look beyond these signposts to examine the heart or soul number of your mate and yourself, for these heart desires remain the same throughout your life span. Look to see if you are both introverts or extroverts. If not, which is the extrovert (go-getter), and which the introvert (retiring). If the woman is the extrovert, would the husband be satisfied with having her be the boss. People in love often find it difficult to listen to reason, but future heartaches could often be avoided if specific warnings were headed. Numerology will tell you what they are, but you must choose your own disposition of them.

Before you take the final step in marriage, check the following steps to determine if you are harmonious or if you will clash frequently.

Step 1: If your heart's desires are the same, then there will be a compelling pull between you, and the tie will strengthen. If both the soul's urges and birthpaths are the same, you will be well-mated.

Step 2: Are your principle numbers similar, complementary, or opposites?
If similar, they will be harmonious.
If the numbers of both are even or odd, they are complementary.
If opposites, one even and the other odd, they will clash.

Step 3: If you have the same destiny, then you will have common interests. You will have more of a chance to be happy since you will enjoy the same type of activity.

Step 4: If your birthpath numbers are the same, you will be attracted to one another both from the business and social standpoint because of similar interests. You have the same lesson to learn, and are found at the same level of intelligence.

Step 5: If your birthdays are in the same concord, your outlook or approach will be the same.

Step 6: If your power numbers are the same, then you will be attracted to one another because you will have the same goal and will be traveling in the same direction.

Step 7: If your personal years are the same, such as both having a six, marriage may be in the air, and uppermost in your mind.

Step 8: Study the character traits and planes of expression. If one is too emotional, it may annoy the other mental partner. A practical person may be discouraged with a mate living on the intuitional or inspirational plane, or vice versa.

Step 9: Look at the pinnacles in connection with your destiny numbers. A pinnacle of nine with a destiny number of seven would not be inducive to a lasting marriage. Marriage ties may be shaky if the destiny numbers are 7, 5, or 9. Notice also if you are both introverts or extroverts.

HOW TO RECOGNIZE YOUR TYPE—
INTROVERT OR EXTROVERT

Numbers are of two types, namely, Introverts and Extroverts. The introverts consist of the odd numbers 1, 3, 5, 7, 9. The extroverts are these numbers 2, 4, 8, 11, 22.

Extroverts, are outgoing. They love life, entertainment, people, society, and companionship. They do not like to be alone, for they want to be seen and heard.

Introverts are students and thinkers. They are often withdrawn, quiet, and reserved. They like to mix in a small group—not a. crowd. While they remain in the background, they constantly observe and listen, gather facts, and weigh them carefully. Their aim is to succeed in their chosen field. Introverts often produce great scientists, artists, and educators.

Most individuals are a combination or mixture of both types of numbers, thus producing balance.

CHART COMPARISONS TO LEARN IF PARTNERS ARE IN SAME
CONCORD—BUSINESS PARTNERS, FRIENDS, ASSOCIATES

Making chart comparisons determines the degree of harmony in partnerships in business associates, also with friends, products, house numbers, and cities. We compare charts to see if the principle numbers are similar, complementary, or opposite.

People born in the same concord are more harmonious than in concords composed of mixed numbers. For example: If your birthday is in the artistic concord of 3-6-9 you will mix best with a person born in the same air concord. Those in the water concord of 1-5-7 will mix best with others in the same scientific concord, while those in the business concord of 2-4-8-11-22 will be harmonious with those born in the fire concord.

Example:

JOHN BOWER	ALFRED SMILEY
June 6	October 12

They would be harmonious as partners providing other numbers are compatable. Business partners would work well together if their destiny numbers were similar. The comparisons hold for business partners and friendships the same as for marriages, as they all are partnerships.

Your destiny or expression indicates your line of opportunity, and is a must in your life. If the destinies of two partners in business are the same, but their inner selves (vowels) differ, this would be good because their ideas will be different, but they will want to express themselves in the same way.

SUMMING UP TO FIND IF YOU ARE HARMONIOUS

If your destiny and birthpath are similar, then you will have the opportunity to fulfill your desires, and your life will be comparatively easy.

Example:

J A C K   P A A R   MAY 1, 1918

1 1 3 2   7 1 1 9   5   1   19

$\dfrac{18}{}$

   -7 $\dfrac{18}{9}$ = 16 = 7 (des-   5   1   10   = 7 (birth-
                             tiny)   path)

If your soul's urge and your destiny are the same, you may do what you desire, but this may cause you to either overdo things or become bored, thus producing a negative effect. In order to counteract this, add the two negative numbers to produce a positive. *Example:* If your soul's urge is five and your destiny is five, add the two fives to produce a positive ten if you become too restless.

Thus:

> Heart's desire   = 5
>
> Personality   = 9
>
> Destiny   = 5
>
> Five plus 5 equals ten.

If one partner has a soul's urge of four and a personality of five with a destiny number of nine, while the other has a soul's urge of three, a personality of six, and a destiny number of nine, they will work well together.

Example:

Mr. A: Heart 4   Mr. B: Heart 3

           Personality .... _5_   Personality ..... _6_

           Destiny   9   Destiny 9

This is a good partnership because they are going in the same direction but they have different desires.

If the destiny or expression number of one partner is found as the birthpath of the other, it establishes the relationship of teacher to pupil. The pupil may in time tire of this situation.

If your soul's urge is higher than your expression, i.e. seven soul and two expression, it indicates that you will have more ideas than you are able to express. This can be remedied by changing your signature to a larger number.

If your expression is higher than your soul's urge, i.e. three soul, seven expression, then it indicates that you have the ability and incentive to express all that is within you. Therefore, you can reach your goal and accomplish your desires.

If your soul's urge is higher than your personality, i.e. nine soul, two personality, it shows that you have greater ability than you have personality. You will be worth cultivating as you will improve upon frequent contact.

If your soul's urge is lower tnan your personality, i.e. three soul, eight personality, it indicates you have a larger parsonality than ideality. You will make a good impression on first acquaintance, but you may later prove you are shallow.

If your soul's urge is higher than your birthpath, i.e. six soul, four birthpath, it indicates that you have the ability to lead or teach those less developed with whom you are associated.

FRIENDSHIPS

Friendships follow the same rule as partners in matrimony. You will usually find that close friends have the same soul's urge, for that is what attracted them to each other in the first place.

PRODUCTS–HOMESITES–CITIES

When naming a new product be sure to take into consideration its needs, or the job it is advertised to do.

For Example:

P A L M O L I V E   = 6 (Domestic commodity serving fam
7 1 3 4 6 3 9 4 5   ily. A soap providing cleanliness.)

$$\underline{42}$$

6

C H E S T E R F I E L D   = 6 (A satisfying cigarette.)
3 8 5 1 2 5 9 6 9 5 3 4

60 = 6

H A M M O N D   O R G A N   = 6 (Music for the home,
8 1 4 4 6 5 4   6 9 7 1 5   an article of beauty.)

$$\underline{32} \qquad \underline{28}$$

5   1

A Y R E S   = 5 (Leader of fashion.)
1 7 9 5 1

$$\underline{23}$$

5

The name of a new real estate addition would be most harmonious if the name totalled six.

Example:

TI MBERCREST   =   6 (A good place to establish
2 9 4 2 5 9 3 9 5 1 2   a home and raise a family.)

51

6

GL E N W O O D   P A R K   = 6
7 3 5 5 5 6 6 4   7 1 9 2

41   19

5   1

B RI A R W O O D   = 6
2 9 9 1 9 5 6 6 4

51

6

CITIES

Does your city want what you have to offer?

If you are unhappy in the city in which you live, and feel that you are constantly missing the boat, then before making a change, think what you want to achieve, and then choose a city which wants (soul's urge) what you have to offer (destiny). If you want experience, choose a city which expresses your birthpath. It will not be easy, but you'll have an opportunity to learn under its influence.

HOW TO TELL IF YOU ARE IN
HARMONY WITH YOUR CITY

Cities and states have their own desires or demands. You must cooperate with them the same as with a partner or relative.

You are in harmony with cities in your own concord. If you plan to move, then ask yourself: Does the city or locality to which I am moving have any of my numbers—destiny, birthpath, soul's urge, or power number? It will be much easier to make a change if you understand its desires and needs. Study the city in which you live. If you want to make a change purely because you feel restless or depressed in it, or have been unsuccessful there, then see what the city desires and try to fulfill its requirements. Perhaps if you offer what it wants, then you may encounter opportunities. However, if for business reasons you must move, then see if you can meet its requirements.

Example:

5	6	= 11 (soul's desire)		9	1	6 = 7 (soul)
N E W	Y O R K			C H I C A G O		

5 5 7 9 2		3 8 3 7
1	9 =	21
6 plus 6 equals 3 (destiny)		3

Total: 7 plus 3 = 10 (destiny)

New York wants inspirational people (11) with ideas (11), who can face the public or limelight and be superior. Cities actually do not have personalities. Its destiny or expression number is three, which means one of self-expression, creativity, and artistic endeavors such as music, art, writing, advertising. It attracts entertainers.

Chicago with the soul's urge of seven desires thinkers, scientists, and analytical people. With the total destiny number of ten, it shows that it wants ana demands originality, leadership, and people who are independent and reliable.

Another example:

$$\frac{9}{6 \qquad 6\ 6}$$

$$\underline{\text{H O L L Y W O O D}} = 3 \quad \text{(a city of entertainment, music self-}$$
$$8 \quad 3 \quad 3 \quad 7 \quad 5 \qquad 4 \qquad \text{expression, dramatics, vacation spot)}$$

$$\frac{30}{3}$$

9 plus 3 equals 3 = Destiny

You are in harmony with cities in your own concord.

Example:

$$\text{J O H N} \qquad \text{A L B E R T} \qquad \text{B R O W N} = 6$$

$$\underline{1\ 6\ 8\ 5} \qquad \underline{1\ 3\ 2\ 5\ 9\ 2} \qquad \underline{2\ 9\ 6\ 5\ 5}$$
$$2 \qquad\qquad 22 \qquad\qquad 27/9$$

BORN: February 9, 1943 = 10

$$2 \qquad 9 \quad 8 \ (1+9)$$

Mr. Brown would be successful in an artistic city totalling 3, 6, 9, since his birthday is on the ninth, or in any city totalling 1-5-7 for his birthpath is ten.

To find the vibration of a city we find the total vowels and expression or destiny number. If either is in harmony with your birthday or birthpath, then it would be a good place in which to move.

$$\frac{6}{6 \quad\quad 1 \quad 5} \; = 12 = 3 \text{ (soul's urge)}$$

F O R T   W A Y N E

6 6 9 2   5 1 7 5 5

23   23

5   5   = 10   (destiny)

Fort Wayne is an air (3) and water (10) city, and would be harmonious for John Albert Brown. His birthday (9) is harmonious with the city soul's urge (3) and his birthpath of 10 the same as that of Ft. Wayne.(10).

WHAT DOES YOUR HOUSE NUMBER MEAN?

If you plan to move to another house, stop to consider what you want and expect from the new house. Houses too have natures, and they like to be themselves. *For example:* If you move into any house with a three (2136 = 3) house number or vibration, you can expect it to be lively and full of company. If, however, you have a seven destiny number and want quietude to rest, and study, then this house could make you very unhappy with its social atmosphere. A five house number (1823) demands freedom, change, and versatility.

If you feel uncomfortable in the house in which you now live, do not move immediately. Instead, try to understand its vibrations just as you would a person, and then attempt to live up to its requirements. For instance, if you move into a house with a four (work, routine) vibration, but you prefer society life (3), then do what is necessary to put the house in order such as cleaning, decorating, and landscaping. After you have fulfilled its requirements, you may be surprised to find that you'll enjoy its atmosphere after all. If you still persist in being unhappy, then it might be feasible to move into a place which meets your own vibrations. Usually, you'll find that the discord lies within yourself.

Remember, even though the house in which you live is not heaven, you should not permit its vibrations to govern your entire life. You are an individualist and you have your own mission to accomplish. Your house number, plus your street number, give a complete meaning to your home, but the house number has a stronger influence.

EXPLANATION OF HOUSE NUMBERS:
LEARN WHAT IS EXPECTED OF YOU

Number 1

If a house number reduces to one, such as (1261), it will appeal to independent individuals who pursue creative and original activities. If these traits are undeveloped, they often fulfill them while living in a number one house. They like to run affairs and be head of committees in the community. They are proud.

Number 2

If a house number reduces to two, such as (12890), this house will attract quiet, dignified people who like to live simply. They are diplomatic and tactful in dealing with neighbors and friends. An arrogant, dictatorial person would not fit in this house. Number twos may enter into lasting partnerships both in business .and in family life.

Number 3

If a house number reduces to three, such as (3693), .this house will bring much joy and happiness to its occupants. It will be a good place to entertain, but care must be exerted lest the occupants spend more than they can afford for pleasure. Creative talent will thrive here.

Number 4

If a house number reduces to four (4963), this house will appeal to very practical people. They are honest, orderly, economical, and not afraid of manual labor. Since they are excellent managers. they are respected and well-liked in the community.

Number 5

If a house number reduces to five (92723), this house will be enjoyed by versatile people who will be on the move constantly. They will not be very domestic, but will do their bit in the community by working on drives and projects. They like action even though it results in turmoil.

Number 6

If a house number reduces to six (3867), this house will attract people who enjoy a close family life. While much responsibility and domestic affairs are ever present, if living constructively, this house will offer its occupants money, love, and comfort. It is a home, not just a house, with artistic interior furnishings and not just a place to sleep. Welfare and community work will come forth from its occupants.

Number 7

If a house number reduces to seven (7288), this house offers rest and quietude to its dwellers. It is a good place in which to further educational pursuits. It will be harmonious for deep thinkers. It is not inducive to wild parties or fun.

Number 8

If a house number reduces to eight (6524), this house will have an atmosphere of importance and success. It may even be a place from which business is conducted. Good judgment and efficiency will be required of its occupants because this is not essentially a domestic home, but one in which the dwellers make a showing or impression on others.

Number 9

If a house number reduces to nine (8766), this house will appeal to those who want to serve and help humanity. This place will be "OPEN HOUSE" to anyone in need. It will also attract lovers of the arts. A number nine house has a universal attraction rather than a personal, for it is based on love and understanding. However, if the occupants are not living constructively, it may bring many disappointments and losses. Therefore, it often is avoided when choosing a house number.

Remember, a house number which reduces to six is harmonious for the entire family. The same principle applies to apartments, for the number of your apartment tells what is expected of you.

You can't change your house number, for it is against the law. If you try hard enough, you and your house can usually be harmonious.

TWENTY

How to Change
Your Name to Benefit You

Your original full name contains your past experiences, character, and destiny. While you may change your name and achieve success, actually you should not do so unless you've outgrown its use through conscious effort. If you have progressed beyond the vibratory effects of your old name, then a new name will give you additional tools with which to work to fulfill your job or any goal.

You've often heard some friend grumble, "My parents didn't give me the right name." This is an ambiguous and erroneous assumption. Your present name was subconsciously impressed on your parents so that you could gain its needed experience.

HOW YOU CAN CHANGE YOUR NAME
FOR A PURPOSE

Every name is good, and most individuals have been named correctly. If you're constantly facing obstacles, having set-backs, and feel uncomfortable when your name is spoken, then it might be feasible to change it. Changing your name will be of no benefit to you if you don't apply what the new name suggests. If the new name is merely a hope chest, tag of identification, or a name plate, then its effects will be weak or negative, for the new name, as well as the original, must be lived up to and developed through hard work.

WHAT DO YOU PLAN TO DO WITH YOUR NEW NAME?

Changing your name is a serious business which should not be attempted by a novice. If you are contemplating on using a pseudonym or pen name, your first consideration should be what you intend to do with it. If you expect to appear before the public, then a long name with difficult spelling and pronunciation could be a deterrent to your success, for a short euphonious, rhythmic name will be more easily remembered and publicized. Remember, in changing your name, many factors must be considered such as your pinnacles, karmic lessons, challenges, and your total birthpath. However, the most important factor is to harmonize your new full name with your birthpath, and be sure it conforms to the odd and even category. If you hope to escape the responsibility of your purpose in life, you might better keep your present name. Even if you change your name, the original name will still be in the background and urge you to gain the necessary experience to fulfill the destiny it chose at birth. Your soul wants to progress in the direction of your total vowels, for that is the urge you brought with you. All you need do is to understand and use your potentials.

An Example of a Change of Name to Gain Beneficial Results Is:

Barbara Stanwyck's original name was Ruby Stevens. She was born on July 16, 1907. We'll now set up these two names and the date of birth with corresponding numerological values:

```
        3               8       = 11

    _____     _____
    1    1   1       1    7

    B A R B A R A   S T A N W Y C K

    2   9 2   9     1 2   5 5   3 2
        22                  18    =   (22 – 9)
                            9
```

7 plus 8 equals 15 equals 6   (Destiny)

$$\frac{1}{\frac{10}{3 \quad 7}} \qquad \frac{1}{\frac{10}{5 \quad 5}} \qquad = 20$$

R U B Y   S T E V E N S

$$\frac{9 \quad 2}{11} \qquad \frac{1 \, 2 \quad 4 \quad 5 \, 1}{\frac{13}{4}} \qquad = (11 + 4)$$

3 plus 5 equals 8 (destiny)

Date of Birth: July   16   1907

$$7 \qquad 7 \qquad \frac{17}{8} \quad = 22 \quad \text{(birthpatn)}$$

With her master birthpath of twenty-two, she needed a stronger and more harmonious name than Ruby Stevens to balance it. While the total of eight in the name of Ruby Stevens is good, it is made up of a vowel total of 20, which would make Barbara Stanwyck shy and retiring and not desirous of appearing before the public in the spotlight. In addition to this, her eight total would have been fine in the business world, but not for an actress or anyone starting out in an artistic field. The new total of six with a master eleven vowel total, obtained from the name of Barbara Stanwyck gave her high ideals or aims, and put her in the artistic field of acting. It also contained the twenty-two total of consonants in her first name of Barbara, giving her another master number to match her total birthpath of twenty-two, which is the largest number possible. The six destiny total of the new name is the same as her pinnacle of six, which indicates a good voice for acting, and for serving the public in an artistic capacity.

I'll give you another example. I would suggest that you not only study it but work it out yourself and then compare it with mine.

Kate Smith was born Kathryn Elizabeth Smith on May 1, 1909.

$$\frac{2}{20}$$

8

| 1 | 7 | 5 | 9 | 1 | 5 | | 9 | = 10 |

K A T H R Y N   E L I Z A B E T H   S MI T H

| 2 | 2 8 9 | 5 | | 3 | 8 | 2 | 2 8 | 1 4 | 2 |

$$\frac{26}{8} \qquad \frac{23}{5} \qquad \frac{15}{6} = 10$$
(1 + 9)

7 plus 7 plus 6 equals (20) destiny

| 6 | 9 | = 6 |

| J | 5 | 9 |

K A T E   S MI T H

| 2 | 2 | 1 4 | 2 8 |

$$\frac{15}{6} = 10$$

10 plus 6 equals 16 = 7 (Destiny)

Date of Birth: May   1   1909

5   1 $\dfrac{19}{10}$ = 7 (birthpath)

When Kathryn Elizabeth Smith changed her name or her signature to Kate Smith, she acquired perfect harmony, for her adopted name of Kate Smith with a total of *seven* destiny is *exactly the same as her birthpath* of *seven*. This gave her additional talents with which to realize her goal in life. She is a perfectionist. The *six* total vowel shows her to have a good voice in speaking or singing. It is much better for her than her original name, which would have made her reticent. Many actors carry the seven total.

Often merely changing the spelling of your name or adjusting the signature by adding an initial *to conform to your birthpath* is sufficient to produce satisfactory results. However, if you can't synchronize your name with your vocation or birthpath, then it is wise to change your name entirely.

WHEN YOU CAN USE ONE NAME ONLY

Occasionally a famous person is known by one name only. In history, Bismark, Mussolini, and Napoleon had this distinction. In literature Shakespeare, and in the arts Rembrandt, are known by only one name. In addition to being famous, their names must be unique and distinctive enough to stand alone.

In the entertainment field Liberace, the famous pianist, is known by his surname only. His full name is:

$$\frac{\overset{1}{10}}{1 \quad 9} \qquad \frac{\overset{3}{21}}{1 \quad 5 \quad 9 \quad 6} \qquad \frac{\overset{2}{20}}{9 \quad 5 \quad 1 \quad 5} = 6$$

WLADZIN   VALENTINO   LIBERACE

$$\frac{5\ 3 \quad 4\ 8 \quad 5}{25 \quad (7)} \qquad \frac{4 \quad 3 \quad |5\ 2 \quad 5}{19 - (10) - (1)} \qquad \frac{3 \quad 2 \quad 9 \quad 3}{17 \quad (8)} = 7$$

8 plus 4 plus 1 = 13 = 4

Date of Birth: May   16   1919 = 14 = 5
               5   7   20(2)

$$\begin{array}{l} \overset{2}{20} \qquad = 2 \\ \text{LIBERACE} \\ \underline{8 \qquad = 8} \\ \qquad\qquad 10 \end{array}$$

His change in name resulted in dropping all but his surname of Liberace (10). His full given name totals four, which is excellent for a politician, government worker, mechanic, or builder, but not for a musician. However, the four will always demand constant hard work from him even though he uses his single surname of Liberace. Also, the full name would be difficult for the public to pronounce, and would not lend itself well for the stage or advertising purposes.

The single name of Liberace (10) is harmonious and in the same concord with his birthday (16), and his birthpath (5), which is in the water or scientific concord of (1-5-7). The ten total of Liberace puts him in a class by himself, for he has an individual style (1), is a showman (10 = 1), and a leader.

Another example of a person using only one name is HILDE-GARDE. Her full name is Hildegarde Loretta Sells. She was born on February 1, 1906. She also is a pianist and entertainer. The present signature of the single name of Hildegarde is in perfect harmony with her birthpath, which is also 10. It indicates an individualist with a pioneering spirit. She is an independent artist with an unusual style.

Example:

$$\frac{2}{20} \quad + \quad \frac{3}{12} \quad + \quad 5 \quad = \quad 10$$

9	5	1	5	6	5	1	5
H I	L D E	G A R	D E	L O R E T T A	S E L L S

HI LDEGARDE   LORETTA   SELLS

8 3 4   7   9 4   3   9   2 2   1   3 3 1

$$\frac{35}{8} \qquad \frac{16}{7} \qquad \frac{8}{8} \; = \; 5$$

10 plus 10 plus 4 equals 24   = 6

Date of Birth: February   1,   1906

$$\frac{2 \qquad 1 \qquad 16}{7} \; = \; 10$$

The symbol used by Hildegarde is long kid gloves. Liberace's symbol is a candelabra. He used his last name, she her first.

$$\frac{2}{20} \qquad\qquad \frac{2}{20}$$

HI L D E G A R D E = 10   L I B E R A C E = 10

8   8

There are many similarities between the two. The vowels, personality and destiny numbers of the last name of Liberace are the same as the first name of Hildegarde.

_____

CHOOSING A NAME FOR A BABY

In analyzing and choosing a name for a baby, you should remember that the last, or surname, is constant and unchangeable. This is not just a custom, but it follows a deep metaphysical law. It reveals the hereditary traits of the *father*. The first name will indicate the individuality, while the middle name will merely strengthen the other qualities. However, if the middle name is the one most commonly used, the reverse will take place. You must consider the fact that if a child is destined due to family connections to follow a certain line such as heading a family business, or a large corporation, or if he follows his father's footsteps as an inventor, actor, politician, or a doctor, you should choose a name vibration which cooperates with the occupation to be followed.

In naming a baby several points should be taken under advisement:

1. The total original given name at birth should be of the same numerical value as the total birthpath number. If this cannot be done, then it should at least harmonize.
2. The first name should complete the concord of the birthday (day of month) such as the 14th or the 21st, not the year or birthdate total.

THE TRIANGLE OR TRINITY METHOD

In choosing a name for a baby, the triangle or trinity is again prominent. The birthdate is at the bottom of the triangle, and it is called the Cornerstone. At the apex or top of the triangle we place the first letter of the first name. At the other base the total value of the first name forms the capstone.

Example:

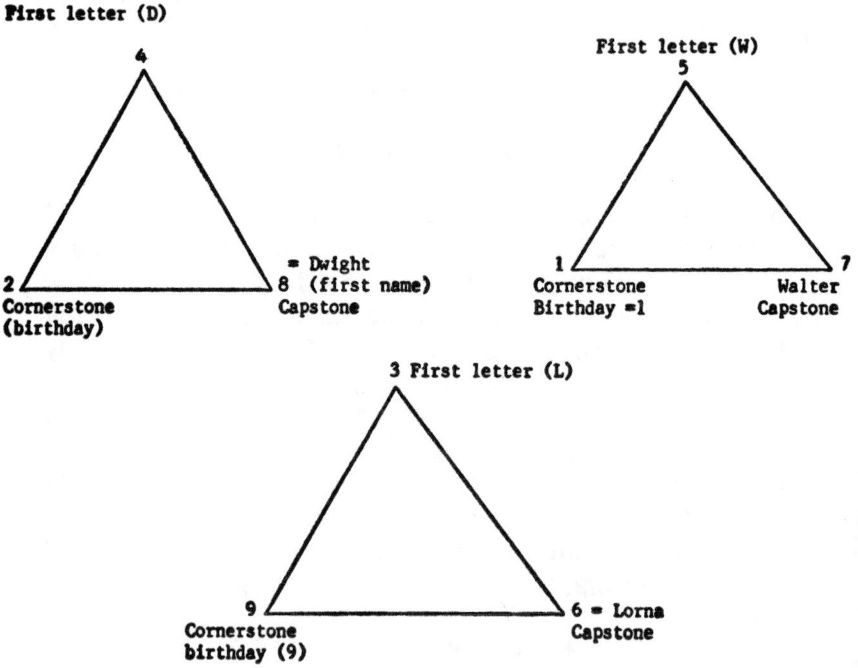

First letter (D)

```
            4
           /\
          /  \
         /    \
        /      \        = Dwight
       /        \       8 (first name)
      2──────────8      Capstone
   Cornerstone   Capstone
   (birthday)
```

First letter (W)

```
            5
           /\
          /  \
         /    \
        /      \
       /        \
      1──────────7
   Cornerstone   Walter
   Birthday =1   Capstone
```

3 First letter (L)

```
            3
           /\
          /  \
         /    \
        /      \
       /        \
      9──────────6  = Lorna
   Cornerstone   Capstone
   birthday (9)
```

Figure 20-1

If a child is born on the 19th of any month he is in the scientific concord of 1-5-7. The first letter of his name should begin with a letter whose value is 5 (W) and the total first name seven (Walter), or the first letter should have a value of seven and the total value should be 5. *Example:* Paul, Eleanor.

If a child is born on the 9th of any month in the artistic concord of 3-6-9, the first letter of his name should reduce to three (L) and the total name value to six (Lorna), or the first letter should be six and the total value three. *Example:* Lorna, Owen.

If a child is born in the fire concord of 2-4-8-11-22 the first letter value should be four (D) if born on the second, and the total name eight (Dwight), or the first letter should value 8 (H) and the total four or twenty-two. *Example:* Virginia, Helen, Marjorie.

While many numerologists prefer to use the triangle method of choosing a first name for a baby, I do not insist anyone master it because I think it is very complicated for a novice to decipher, plus the fact that it limits their choice of a name. I use it myself because it is accurate and scientific in its delineation, and it gives additional points for consideration, but it is not the final word. After you have chosen the right first name, the total single digit must be incorporated into the full given name by adding the surname, which is hereditary, and the middle name, and harmonizing the total of all the names with the birthpath.

CHOOSING A NAME FOR A BABY IS THE
JOB OF AN EXPERT

Naming a baby, or changing a signature, should require the services of an expert numerologist, but often a layman changes or selects a name without having any conception or knowledge of what is involved in this sacred undertaking. My belief is that your destiny is mapped out for you at birth. Since you chose your prospective parents, they should have the responsibility of naming you. You came to fulfill the purpose which is written in your destiny, or full name. This should harmonize with your birthpath.

The following nine steps will aid you in selecting a name for a baby:

Step 1. Reduce the last name to a single digit. (You will need the surname which has already been established.)

Step 2. Make two lists of first name preferences—male and female.

Step 3. Reduce the first names on both lists to single digits.

Step 4. Compile two lists of middle names of both sexes according to preferences.

Step 5. Reduce these middle names to a single digit for future use.

Step 6. Wait until the baby is born to make the final decision of a name.

Step 7. When born, add birthdate (day, month, and year) and reduce to a single digit.

Step 8. Add surname total to one of the first and middle names you chose until you get the same reduced total as the birthpath.

Step 9. If you cannot produce perfect harmony or the same total, then harmonize the name with the birthpath, meaning, put them in the same concord, such as 3-6-9. *Example:* If the baby is born on the 9th, the name total should be *three* or *six*, that is, if you cannot make it *nine.*

TWENTY-ONE

The Kabala and Abracadabra Numerological Methods of Predictions

HOW TO SET UP THE INVERTED PYRAMID

The inverted pyramid or triangle is used to set up the magical formula of the Abracadabra. Each line is one figure or letter less than the line above it. This method also uses the nine digits for its interpretation.

The triangle method had its origin in the great pyramid of Gizeh in Cheops, Egypt, which contains all of the secrets of the ages. It is one of the keys which unlocks the door to wisdom. Another method of preserving truths was concealed in Numerology (numbers) and Astrology (planets), while still another was incorporated into the Tarot cards. Records of esoteric secrets were hidden in the secret passages of the pyramids.

KABALA

A Kabala embodies secret information which may be revealed in a numerical, literal, or hieroglyphical form A kabalist interprets the symbolism of numbers. His method demonstrates the fact that numbers have a significance apart from our recognized numerical value, and they furnish the key to understanding the world.

A KABALA WITH A KEY FOR YOU TO USE

A few kabalas are still in use for divination purposes by numerologists, but most of them have become obsolete due to the

203

fact that the keys to interpret them have been lost. Fortunately, years ago I acquired a very ancient method with its corresponding key. It is not my delineation. I believe it was given to me by Orcella Rexford, a numerologist who has been dead for many years. Since she was unable to interpret it herself, she offered it to me. So far I have never seen a Kabala in print with its key. I have revised it so that it can be understood by you. I do not use it in my predictions. If you are sufficiently interested and diligent in deciphering it, the information may prove to be very valuable I was told by a psychic that when understood the Kabala with its key is the most accurate method devised for predicting the future. I'm now giving the secret to you. I'm most anxious for you to see how this system of interpreting numbers is done through the scientific law of order. The interpretation parallels that of the Tarot.

Figure 21-1 is a sample of the inverted pyramid or triangle. I'll first use numbers to demonstrate the system. Note how the third line of figures is structured by adding 1 + 2 = 3 to form the underlying "3" etc.

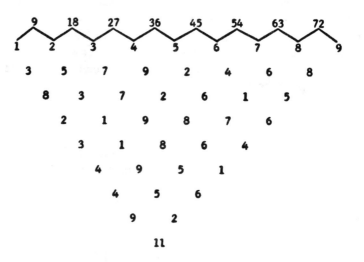

Figure 21-1

I'll now substitute letters of a name for the nine digits. Using the fictitious name of Dorothy Miller, I'll start with her first name, and finally her last name until all of the nine digits have been used.

To arrive at the apex or bottom you add adjacent digits to form the line immediately below it. All compound numbers are reduced to a single digit such as 11 = 2; 12 = 3. The first letter of Dorothy, namely, D (4) plus the second letter of O (6) = 10 = 1. See Figure 21-2.

Thus:

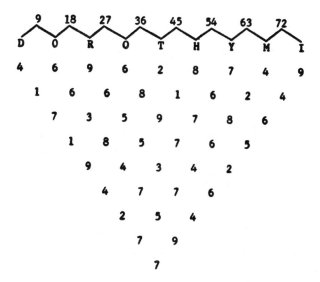

Figure 21-2

Number seven is at the base of this inverted triangle.

Using the nine digits I'll now set up another name with a double first name: SUE ELLEN ALLEN. See Figure 21-3.

Five is a the base of the pyramid for Sue Ellen Allen.

HOW YOU CAN INTERPRET THE PYRAMID METHOD

The number at the bottom of the triangle or inverted pyramid is one of special significance, and should be the first number to be

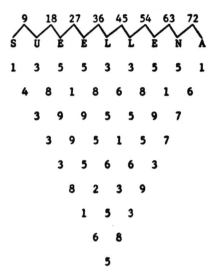

Figure 21-3

read. *Example:* 11 (2) is at the bottom of the first triangle (Figure 21-1). Turn to the table to learn the meaning. Number 7 is at the bottom of the second pyramid (Figure 21-2), and 5 at the bottom of the third (Figure 21-3).

MEANING OF NUMBERS AT THE BOTTOM
OF THE PYRAMID

1.	Alone, independence, recognition.
2, or 11.	Doormat, victim of circumstances.
3.	Society, pleasure, indecision, gain. Need of silence.
4, or 22.	Plodding, hard work, mass production. Need tact. (22) Public office.
5.	Travel, changes, restlessness, unexpected, fickleness.
6.	Love, marriage, family, responsibility, peace, loyalty.
7.	Analyst, skeptic, student, critic, psychic.
8.	Money, delays, justice, business, expansion, illness.
9.	Losses, disappointments, religion, sympathy, big money.

GENERAL MEANING OF NUMBERS OF THE ABRACADABRA

1.	Honor, loss.
15-19	Love, marriage, pregnancy.

4-9	Death of male.
5-8	Death of female.
11	Publicity, partnerships, groups, cooperation, caution needed. (Partnerships equal eleven)
5-6	Partnership—marriage, if 2 connected (choice). If business partner, he's quiet, agreeable, and resourceful.
3-8	Partnership—marriage of intellect . . . generous, religious, literary, and extravagant.
4-7	Partnership—good for business. Can handle money and people.
2-9	Partnership—dangerous, deceit, intrigue, insincerity
18	Adverse
15	Personal—affects you personally.
19	Connubial—affects two people, home.
9 and 2 (7's)	Something hidden from you (money or secret).
7	Water, study, travel, protection.
1-8-1	Limited circumstances.
18 over 9	With pin point 5—money through death.
13 over 4	Death.
14	Public.
6	Voice.
3	People.
6-9	Change of home, home affairs.
88 over 7	Tragic accident.
2 (5's and 9)	Confusion, gossip.
3 (5's)	Travel.
Circle of 5's	Scandal.
16	Accident.
5 and 3	Travel—long (5); short (3); if right (5) west, if 7 (near water).
44 over 8	Make name known yourself.
17	Finances.
9 and 2 (4's)	Contact people of high position.
29	Need to guard against false friends.
3 (9's)	Acquire money—loss if with 29 through fraud.
9 and 2 (3's)	Money gained through friends.
6 and 9	Some change in regard to home or purchase of furniture.
33 over 6	Everything provided for.

THE ABRACADABRA METHOD

In charting a name and building up the cycles and spans, the following aspects can be found under the letters of the name and the combination of numbers. It should be remembered that there are but sixty-four combinations of numbers and that any number over sixty-four should be reversed. Thus, sixty-five becomes fifty-six and the information regarding fifty-six is noted.

FOLLOW THIS ABRACADABRA TABLE

1 or 10

One or *ten* indicates a recognition or honor in your life, depending on your age and position. *One* or *ten* foretells a loss. This could be financial or personal, such as the death of someone in the family, a relative, associate, or a friend. When an honor enters your life, it usually is coupled with a personal loss. *Ten* is the number of action, independence, aggression, and often conceit and arrogance. When *ten* is strongly influenced by eighteen over nine, you can count on a business loss through competition or intrigue.

Example:

> If you have 18/9 on the left side and one on the right, the 91/10 it produces is read as 19 (reversed) and is interpreted as 10 because (1 plus 9 equals 10).

2 or 11

Two or *eleven* indicates partnership opportunities or an amalgamation of your business with other firms. In a woman's chart it may mean close association with one or more couples of which the husbands are business partners. *Eleven* also indicates help and interest of others in you. If you are working for a firm and an *eleven* shows in your chart, it shows cooperation plus someone's interest in your advancement and success. There are various combinations of 11's.

> (2-9) An *eleven* arrived at through two and nine or 29/11 points to an insincere person with a brilliant personality. Beware of this type, for he'll use intrigue to gain his objective without paying any money. Never enter into a partnership with such a person.
> (3-8) An *eleven* arrived at through three and eight shows a person who is generous, religious, intelligent, and literary, but he may be

extravagant. He may be an organizer but quarrelsome.

(4-7) An *eleven* arrived at through four and seven means an agreeable, successful business partner able to handle people and money. He's an excellent broker or banker.

(5-6) An *eleven* arrived at through five and six shows he's quiet, resourceful, and agreeable. He would be a good marriage partner. This partner is helpful and may reach high places in business.

Elevens tend to publicity. In association with many 13's over 4 they may develop into scandal. *Eleven* injects life into groups, but it may be nervousness. Caution is also advised in dealings.

3.

A *three,* or any combinations of numbers producing a *three,* indicates much gain and pleasure, and success will come easily. The *three* calls for silence in plans and ideas which could be advantageous. A *three* denotes a sense of humor, society, friends, and enjoyment. *Three* indicates establishing of a home and having children. If *three* shows up beyond the age of production, this could mean adoption or care due to the death of the parents. If there are several threes and a nine, especially eighteen over nine, then there is danger of a libel suit. Again be careful what you say, as *three* rules words.

4.

A *four* indicates the public through work. This may mean you'll have something to do with mass production such as is sold in a department store. Many *fours* in a chart indicate delay, where tact and patience are necessary. *Fours* show opposition. *Four,* especially if under twenty-two, indicates the possibility of running for public office. If a *four* occurs in your date of birth or name, this is almost sure to happen. Thirteen over four, and twenty-two over four, are associated with death. The twenty-two indicates the possibility of a public funeral with tribute paid.

5.

A *five* shows movements, and surprises of a quick and sudden nature. Fourteen over five shows you before the public (1, person,

4, public). If the arrangement is 41 it means you are serving the public. The masses (4) come first, and you (1) play second fiddle. Fourteen over five means you are in the spotlight. The more fourteens over fives, the more chances there are for this to happen. Twenty-three over five shows protection of some person of influence. His advice can be followed to your advantage. Many *fives* denote trickery. Watch so that you are not cheated. Many *fives* indicate restlessness and indecision, and many changes. Don't make too many promises. *Five* shows love of travel, adventure, and gambling.

6.

A *six* shows responsibilities, domestic relations, love affairs, and servants. Many *sixes* slow down affairs. *Six* augurs peace and harmony. Too many *sixes* may indicate heart trouble. If a person is single, *six* implies indecision in marriage or a choice of a suitor. If married, it may mean deliberation over separation or a divorce. The opposite sex is involved. Be sure you are just. Thirty-three over six is very fortunate, and shows everything is provided for you. It usually shows you can help others, for you have more than you need.

7.

A *seven* shows mysterious forces in the foreground. It means it is a good time for expansion in the spiritual realm. If you live up to your highest ideals you will not suffer. Under a *seven* strange contacts will be made. It is intuitive with psychic experiences and strange dreams.

Seven indicates responsibilities you assume even though they are not forced upon you. Don't let others make a goat of you. *Seven* brings overseas travel. *Seven* is a good time to cater to women of influence. The *seven* span is of a serious nature bringing a desire to study, meditate, and be alone. It denotes vision and advanced ideas.

8.

An *eight* affects your material or physical side. It indicates nealth, death, and legacies. *Eight* denotes delays and disappointments, for there will be obstacles. You will gain by not pushing or driving yourself and others. Justice is the keynote. Forty-four over eight means the opportunity to make your name known and gain a reputation. Many *eights* indicate delays, also the danger of a prolonged illness.

9.

A *nine* shows development of affairs on a large scale, and a big money making span. Much energy will be expended, and emotional experiences will be encountered. You must be on the alert for underhanded dealings, for the larger your interests are, the greater will be the competition, intrigue, and treachery, not by you but by others who aim to destroy you. A *nine* suggests great responsibilities both in business and the home. Domestic relationships could be at a low ebb leading even to a separation or a divorce, especially if followed by an *A, J,* or an *S.* In a *nine* span you must guard against fires, explosions, and accidents, especially

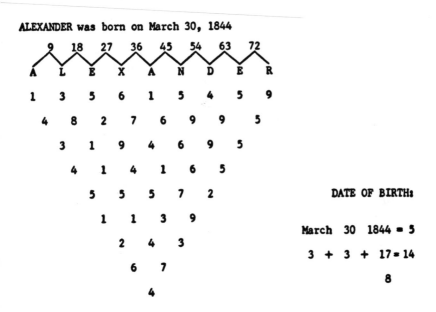

ALEXANDER was born on March 30, 1844

9	18	27	36	45	54	63	72
A	L	E	X	A	N	D	E	R
1	3	5	6	1	5	4	5	9
4	8	2	7	6	9	9	5	
3	1	9	4	6	9	5		
4	1	4	1	6	5			
5	5	5	7	2				
1	1	3	9					
2	4	3						
6	7							
4								

DATE OF BIRTH:

March   30   1844 = 5

3 + 3 + 17 = 14

8

Figure 21-4

in a *nine* year of *nine* year cycle. It also shows need for caution in speech in order to avoid law suits. It's not wise to make an enemy under a *nine*. *Nine* represents money and its problems, and also unwise dealings with the opposite sex. Eighteen over nine shows many difficulties and even tragedy.

Notice: By this time you evidently have noticed that regardless of which method is used (Kabala or mine) the basic interpreting is the same. This is because they stem from the cosmic alphabet which has existed since the beginning of time.

We'll now set up a name and then interpret the meaning by means of the Kabala with its inverted triangle. See Figure 21-4.

A, the first letter of the alphabet, has a value of *one.* This number shows that during the first nine years of Alexander's life his parents made a fresh start in which new interests, new scenes, and friends were experienced. This could mean that when he was between 3½ and 4½ years of age his parents moved, either from a foreign country, or from one part of our country to another. *A,* at the beginning of a name, in combination with *L* or three might denote the death (13) of one or both parents, or their separation through divorce. Something in Alexander's life occurred which placed him in a position of being alone (1). He is called upon to develop himself with perhaps little help from others. At the age of 4 he came with his father and his stepmother to America from Europe. Here the loneliness of the one was experienced because of a resentfulness between him and his stepmother. Being independent (A-1) he would not let her get close to him.

When he was 3½ his real mother died. Note the combination of *A* and *L* (1 and 3 = 13) the grim reaper or death number in his life. Then his father married his present stepmother, and they came to America.

In studying the Abracadabra we note the *three* of the month (ruler of the first cycle) in combination with the *one* of *A* making *thirteen.* The *three* of March rules the home, child, and the family. Study the numbers from birth through 4½, the downhill span of the letter *A.* The final number is *four,* through the total of *six* and *seven* (13-4). The third letter from the top in the first half span is 31 (13 influence). The citizen (1) is back of the family (3), which shows that the family came first and not the child. The *three* of March, and the *one* of *A* gives *thirty-one.* The fifth number from *A* is 5, going downhill, arrived at through the *forty-one,* again placing him behind the group (4) and not before the public. *Five* indicates change and travel, while *four* signifies movement.

Note the *six* second from the bottom number *four*. Here we find love, marriage, and the mother. Right above it is the *two* derived from *eleven* which shows a partnership. Note that the *two* (which rightfully should be an *eleven*) is wedged in between the *five* and *six*, meaning change in partnership through love and marriage. One may assume that there was considerable opposition to the change if not the marriage.

The years from 4½ to 9 in the name indicate that there was routine, system, monotony, and work. Between 8 and 9 there was a change of residence within the community. The *L* (3) shows travel. This plus the *three* of March gives a double *three* or *thirty-three*, an excellent combination showing that everything was provided for him. This double Jupiter also suggests additional children.

Around 12½ to 13½ the double *three* also indicates the possibility of twins, or one child following closely behind the other. Again, between the ages of 17 and 18 another child was born.

It is interesting to note that the vowels of the name Alexander total *twelve* or *three*, suggesting that he would naturally have contact with children, and since *twelve* is the number of sacrifice, he would likely have this experience. Thus, when other children were born to his parents he felt isolated from the others Notice the *A* and the second *A* in his name.

Between 17 and 18 he ran away from home and entered the army. Note the oncoming vibration *E* and its number *five* showing change, travel, freedom, and adventure. *E* in association with the *three* of the month equals *eight*, suggesting obstacles and even death.

Alexander was wounded in battle and lay in a hospital. After the war he came to Chicago and went to work to build his fortune. He was very successful in the candy business. Notice the vowels in candy (8) and the vowels in business (8), which may account for his entering business for himself.

Between 26 and 27 he married, shown by the numbers 5-6 or *two* or *eleven*. This denotes a fine partner and a real helpmate.

The *ten* arrived at through *nineteen* at the same period as the marriage indicates the death of an elderly person (19 = old age), and the *ten* through *fifty-five* (double 5) shows the death of a middle-aged person which came very quickly. *Ten's* indicate some honor.

Between 35 and 36 at the close of the *X* (6) in combination with the *three* of *thirty*, there was financial success through a business. The years of marriage through 36 were fortunate years which brought him in contact with many people (9) through social activities (3) (30), and harmonious, peaceful associations, (6). At 35 to 36 the candy business was given up and he became manager of a large Club House and Concert Hall. Here we must take into consideration the *three* of the month, the *thirty* of the day, and the *three* of the vowels. *Three* rules music, art, literature, dancing, and the theater. Thus it is discernible that his interests gravitated to the lighter side of life, and he became a host.

Between 39½ and 40½ at the peak of the second *A*, there was loss in the sudden death of his wife (1 of *A* and 3 of 30) = 13, which reduces to *four*, meaning the grim reaper.

Below the letter *A* we have 7-6; 4-1; 1-3; 6-7, in a direct straight line ending in 67-4 at the apex or bottom of the Abracadabra.

From 40½ to 45 he was alone (A-1), and between 44 and 45 in the most successful span of his life, he moved from the Club building with his eight children. The year of birth (1844 = 17 = 8) suggests a new residence in the same community.

The *five* of *N* shows freedom and friendly aspects which might have augured a second marriage (*N* is the marriage letter), but the children objected. The *N* is associated with the 30 of the birthday totalling *thirty-five* or *eight*, meaning disappointments, delays, or obstacles.

Between 48½ and 49½ we have this line-up: N-5-9-9-5. Here we see the cause for not marrying was that he was experiencing mental and emotional upsets while debating the advisability of marriage. Finally he decided not to marry because of the children. The indecision is noted in the *fives*, and the *nines* show increased emotionalism.

From 54 through 63 he was under the *four* of *D* and the 4 of 44. This combination (44) is fortunate, for he made his name known. He had success in the wine business selling glass for glass and bottle for bottle (44-8). He made a fortune (8) during this period.

Between 57½ and 58½ notice the triple *nine*, the grand trine of Mars denoting a windfall. He sold his business at a huge profit and retired. The years from 63 through 72 offered much freedom (5) and travel.

Alexander died at the age of 80-81. Notice the sudden death numbers, and the 6-7 or 13-4 or the death number at the bottom of the Abracadabra. His funeral, shown by the four of 1844 and R (18th letter) equalling *twenty-two*, shows recognition and tribute paid to him.

TWENTY-TWO

How to Set Up and Read a Complete Numeroscope

Setting up a chart can be compared with drawing a map of the United States. Within each of the individual states you insert the capital as highlights. Other cities, which are subordinate to the capitals, are then added. The same is true of numerology.

When charting or mapping out a numeroscope you record your main centers such as your Soul's Urge, your Personality, your Destiny, and your Birthpath. In addition, you incorporate other points of importance such as your Pinnacles, Challenges, Power Number, Planes of Expression, Universal and Personal vibrations, and the Karmic lessons. When you have all of the facts recorded on your chart, you should examine them thoroughly to weigh and balance your information accurately before you arrive at a decision.

Since you now have had the opportunity to read, and I hope study and apply the directions given in the various chapters, I shall figure several numeroscopes as examples to show you how you incorporate the knowledge you gained into one complete whole in order to do and interpret a numeroscope.

The foremost value of numerology is in reavealing the destiny of each individual. Your purpose in life is disclosed in the symbols of the full name given at birth. It shows what experiences you must meet and master. Your total birthpath states what grade you are now in. The birthday gives the talents you have previously earned, and which will serve now as tools to fulfill your destiny. Your soul chose a day of birth to best enable you to meet the requirements of the grade you were entering.

In setting up a chart and interpreting it, the following procedure should be followed:

Step 1:   Destiny: Figure the full given name at birth to find what you must do or be.

Step 2:   Soul's Urge: What you desire most to be, do, or have.

Step 3:   Personality: *nalyze it to find how you appear to others.

Step 4:   Present signature: Does it harmonize with your birthpath?

Step 5:   Birthday: Talents you bring with you at birth.

Step 6:   Birthpath: What grade you are in, and what you must learn.

Step 7:   Power number: Your opportunity or last chance to reach a goal.

Step 8:   Pinnacles: Signposts or experiences you cannot avoid.

Step 9:   Challenges: What you lack and must cultivate.

Step 10:   Planes of Expression: What type or temperament are you?

Step 11:   Karmic lessons: Missing digits, also talents.

Step 12:   Age digit: Additional aspects during a year.

Step 13:   Concords: To determine harmony.

Step 14:   Universal cycles: Universal years, months, and days.

Step 15:   Personal years, months, and days.

Step 16:   Letter transits: Number of letters in your name

Step 17:   Key to character

Step 18:   Predictions.

SAMPLE NUMEROSCOPE OF HEATHER CLAUDIA BALLINGER

(Interpretation of her chart)

(You can follow the mechanics of charting below through reference to previous chapters in this book.)

```
   11   +        5  +             o  = (11 + 11) =  22   (Soul's Urge)

   11            14               15
 5 1     5         1 3   9 1    1    9     5

 H E A T H E R   C L A U D I A   B A L L I N G E R

 8     2 8   9   3 3      4      2   3 3   5 7   9

   27            10               29
   9     +       1        +       11  =  (11 + 10) = (11 − 10) (Personality)
                                               3
   11    +       6        +        8  =  (11 + 5) = (11 − 5) (Destiny)
                                               7
   11    +       6 =                     (11 + 6) (Soul's Urge)
                                               8
```

HEATHER BALLINGER

9	11	= (11 – 9)	= 11	(Personality)
11	+ 8	= (11 + 8)		(Present signature)
		10		

Birthday = 3 = Date of birth: November 3, 1940

Power number = 8 (Destiny 7, plus birthpath 1 = 8)

$$11 + 3 + 5 = (11 - 8 = 10) \text{ (birthpath)}$$

Challenges = Chief or main = 1; additional = 3. See Figure 22-1.

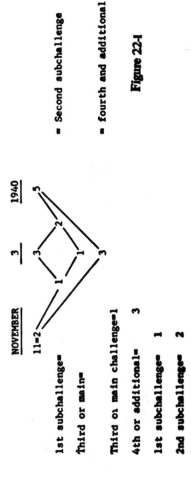

NOVEMBER 3 1940

11=2

1st subchallenge= = Second subchallenge

Third or main=

Third or main challenge=1

4th or additional= 3 = fourth and additional

1st subchallenge= 1

2nd subchallenge= 2

Figure 22-1

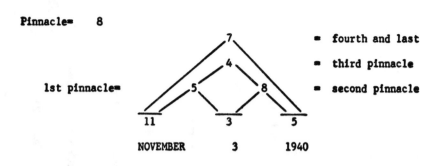

Pinnacle=   8

1st pinnacle=

NOVEMBER   3   1940

= fourth and last

= third pinnacle

= second pinnacle

Figure 22-2

Pinnacles:

1   to   26   = 5

27   to   36   = 8

37   to   46   = 4

47   on   = 7

HEATHER   CLAUDIA   BALLINGER

8 5 1 2 8 5 9   3 3 1 3 4 9 1   2 1 3 3 9 5 7 5 9

Planes of Expression; Emotional and Mental = (See name above.)

Mental   = 6   (Number of 1's and 8's)

Physical   = 5   (Number of 4's and 5's)

Emotional   = 7   (Number of 2's, 3's, and 6's)

Intuitive   = 5   (Number of 7's and 9's)

Karmic Lessons: (Missing digits and talents: See name on p. 220.

No. of 1's = 4
No. of 2's = 2
No. of 3's = 5 (talents)
No. of 4's = 1
No. of 5's = 4
No. of 6's = 0 (missing digit)
No. of 7's = 1
No. of 8's = 2
No. of 9's = 4

Age digit = 9 (If calendar date is March 3, 1972)

Concords: Artistic (3–6–9)

Universal year = 1972 = 10 = 1
Universal day = 7 (If calendar date is 3/3/72)

Personal year = 6 (1972 + 2 + 3);
Personal day = 3 (If calendar date is 3/3/72)

Name cycle = 23 (letters in name, reduced = 5)

Key to character = 5

Predictions = 23, 22, 19, 23.

You are figuring the chart on March 3, 1972

1971 (OVERTONE)	First period (Nov. 3-March 3)	Second period (March 3-July 3)	Third period (July 3-Nov. 3)
14	1971	1971	1971
1985 = 23	31	10	5
	2002 = 22	1981 = 19	1976 = 23

OVERTONE = 23; First period = 22; Second period = 19; Third period = 23

INTERPRETATION OF HEATHER'S CHART FOR YOU

The total destiny number of Heather Claudia Ballinger is (11 + 5) with a reduced total of seven. The total name is Heather (11 + 9 = 11), plus Claudia (5 + 10 = 15 = 6), plus Ballinger (6 + 11 = 17 = 8) which adds to twenty-five (11 + 6 + 8 = 25 = 7). Within her name is her soul's urge number of twenty-two comprised of the vowels (11 + 5 + 6 = 11 + 11 = 22). Her personality or consonants total is three (9 + 1 + 11 = 11 + 10 = 3) reduced.

Her destiny number of (11-5 = 7) reveals both her purpose in life and her opportunity. This means that she should study diligently to acquire much knowledge, skill, and wisdom (7), for she is destined to be a teacher (7), thinker, analyst, or an authority in a technical line (7). The (11-5) total indicates that she is most likely to have unusual experiences even delving into the mysteries of life, and uncovering psychic or scientific facets. This is the number of the lone wolf (7). She must learn to discriminate between the real facts (truth), and what is superficial or false. She may even be thought aloof and strange by the majority. She is a perfectionist (7), and could succeed in research. This is a difficult destiny to fulfill.

Her soul's urge of twenty-two composed of two elevens, shows that she is an old soul with very high ideals. She wants to be an inspiration to others (11-11), appearing in the limelight. She might even aspire to be a foreign diplomat or ambassador (22). The danger of having such a large soul's number is that unless she lives up to its huge demands of the master number twenty-two, it will revert to a four, its lesser aspect, which would limit her to being a hard worker and plodder. Most individuals with a twenty-two soul's urge only live up to its reduced aspect of four, thus aspiring to be a clerk, domestic, accountant, or in the manufacturing or contracting business.

Her personality number of (11-10 = 3) means she appears to others as a jovial individual, interested in the social whirl. Her soul's desire is the opposite of the false face she portrays to others, for she actually is a deep thinker and a perfectionist. She is a fluent talker (3), and makes a good impression as well as being attractive and a well dressed individual (5).

Heather Claudia Ballinger has chosen the present signature of heather Ballinger (11-8 = 10). It means she should succeed in life for the signature is in perfect harmony with her birthpath (11-8 = 10). Her original full name will always remain in the background and demand fulfillment. While it is not as perfect a signature as she now uses, it is harmonious. According to her chart she has a desire to succeed in business. Her personality number of eleven is inspirational, and shows that she is magnatic in appeal. The destiny of her new signature of (11-8 = 10) indicates she must learn to be independent and be a leader.

Heather Ballinger's birthpath of November 3, 1940 gives her a total of (11-8 = 10). She is now in the tenth grade in the school of life. A ten is ten times stronger than a one. It shows she is an old soul, for she has covered the gamut of the single digits and is now launching on the double numbers of the life path. The divisions of the total indicate that she has in a pervious lifetime made an outstanding success in business. Now her life path number indicates that she must learn to be very independent. She must guard against being lazy, arrogant, and dictatorial. The birthpath total of (11 + 8 = 19) is a karmic number, which means that "as she sows so shall she reap" more than any other number. This is both good and bad. She must learn to be a creator, pioneer, and originator. She may have been born in a family where she has been forced to be dependent.

Her birthday on the third states she has the talent of self-expression in writing, speaking, or acting. Therefore, she has the tools to fulfill her destiny number of (11-5 = 7). She has a keen intellectual mind with a vivid imagination. Her job is to teach others. She could succeed as a teacher, writer, missionary, lawyer, or occultist, or be a specialist in any governmental field requiring diplomacy. She could even be a master builder (22) both nationally and internationally, a philanthropist, or a leader of the international set.

Her Power number of eight (destiny plus birthpath) shows that in her later life span she should be honored for her executive ability, authority, and courage. She can be a successful business woman.

Her present pinnacle (a signpost she can't avoid) of eight shows that from twenty-seven to thirty-six she is under a big business pinnacle. It could mean working for the public or owning a business. She has the ability to organize (8) her work.

Her main challenge is one, with an additional challenge of three effective in later life. This means she must learn to stand on her own feet (1). She is apt to be bossed by relatives if she does not assert her independence. The three shows a possibility of becoming interested in too many things. Her main challenge of one coincides with the lesson of (10) of her birthpath, which she must develop.

Looking at her planes of expression, she approaches all problems emotionally and mentally rather than physically or intuitively. She has seven numbers on the emotional plane, and six on the mental. She is a well-balanced individual.

Her missing digit of six, which is a karmic lesson, reveals that she came into this world lacking a desire to assume responsibility, which she avoided in a previous incarnation. She will be forced to carry a heavy load, possibly the care of a family, home, or old people. Until she learns to face, and not sidestep responsibility, it will constantly creep up as a hindrance.

Since this chart is figured on March 3, 1972 her age digit would be nine covering the year 1972, for she would be both thirty-one (4) and thirty-two (5) in the year 1972. Nine is a finishing period. She should not start anything new this year, but clean up leftovers.

She belongs to the artistic concord of 3-6-9, for her birthday is on the third.

Her universal cycle will be three, the day or middle cycle, for she is thirty-one. Each cycle has a duration of twenty-seven years. The three cycle is creative for her in that new ideas will crop up.

While the universal year (1972) will be one for her, her personal year will be six $(11 + 3 + 1 = 6)$. The one means much action and new ventures, while the six indicates responsibilities connected with the community. This could be a year for her to marry. While the Universal day is seven (March 3, 1972), the personal day for her will be three (March (3) plus day (3) plus year $(6) = (3 + 3 + 6 = 3)$.

Her name cycle is twenty-three, for she has twenty-three letters in her entire original name. The reduced cycle is five. This means that every fifth year will be one of minor importance, while every twenty-third year (or multiples of 23) will be a major year for her which should bring important events either good or bad.

Her key to character is five, which shows her to be restless wanting constant change. She may travel much in her life. Her sex urge may also be strong.

In figuring the predictions for the year, you begin with her birthday on November 3, 1971 and run for a year to November 3, 1972. If the chart is set up on March 3, 1972 or any time during the year 1972 before her birthday, the interpreter must use the previous year in his computation.

The overtone for the entire year is twenty-three. This indicates many changes. It is a peculiar vibration with high tension and nervousness. Often an illness occurs and a doctor is needed. It can mean new contacts and even travel. Legal affairs such as settling an estate may be encountered.

The first period of twenty-two, in combination with the overtone of twenty-three, indicates a decision of major importance must be made. When an individual is under the influence of a twenty-two he is so vacillating that his judgment is not to be trusted. He should consult an expert for advice in the field in question. The indecision could be about poor health, travel, or settling of an estate. This period from March 3 to July 3, 1972 is governed by the nineteen. With thy overtone of twenty-three it suggests a strange change of some sort and often legal affairs. It is the beginning of good years, and is a favorable period.

The third period from July 3 to November 3, 1972 is governed by the 23-23 combination. The meaning is about the same as the overtone. It can mean success and protection, but it usually means the possibility of an illness. Travel may be on the agenda.

SAMPLE OF NUMEROSCOPE
OF
MARTHA RAYE

(Interpretation of her chart)

The comedian Martha Raye's full given name at birth is Margie Yvonne Reed. She was born on August 27, 1916.

$$\frac{6}{15} \quad + \quad \frac{11}{11} \quad + \quad \frac{1}{10} \quad = (11 + 7) \text{ (Soul's Urge)}$$
$$9$$

$$\overline{1 \quad 9\ 5} \quad \overline{6 \quad 5} \quad \overline{5\ 5}$$

M A R G I E   Y V O N N E   R E E D

$$\underline{4 \quad 9\ 7} \qquad \underline{7\ 4 \quad 5\ 5} \qquad \underline{9 \qquad 4}$$

$$\frac{20}{2} \quad + \quad \frac{21}{3} \quad + \quad \frac{1\ 3}{4} \quad = \quad 9 \quad \text{(Personality)}$$

$$8 \quad + \quad 5 \quad + \quad 5\ (1+8) = 9 \quad \text{(Destiny)}$$

$$\frac{2}{1 \qquad 1} \quad \frac{6}{1 \quad 5} \qquad\qquad = \quad 8 \quad \text{(Soul's Urge)}$$

M A R T H A   R A Y E

$$\underline{4 \quad 9\ 2\ 8} \qquad \underline{9 \quad 7}$$

$$\frac{23}{5} \qquad\qquad \frac{16}{7} \qquad = 12 \quad = \quad 3 \quad \text{(Personality)}$$
$$=$$

$$7 \quad + \quad 4 \qquad = 11 \quad = \quad 11 \quad \text{(Present}$$
$$\text{Signature)}$$

Date of Birth: August   27   1916

$$8 \ + \ 9 \ + \ 8 \ = 25 = \quad 7 \quad \text{(Birthpath)}$$

Birthday= 27th

Power number= 7

Challenge= 0   AUGUST   27   1916

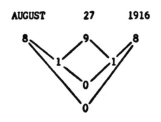

st subchallenge=   Second subchallenge

                                                       Third and main challenge

                                                       Fourth challenge

Figure 22-3

Pinnacle=   7

                                              ● fourth pinnacle

                                              ● third and chief pinnacle

First pinnacle=   ● second pinnacle

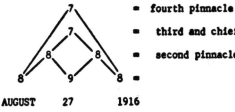

                    AUGUST   27   1916

Figure 22-4

Pinnacles:

1	to	29	= 8
30	to	39	= 8
40	to	49	= 7
50	on		= 7

M A R G I E   Y V O N N E   R E E D

4 1 9 7 9 5   7 4 6 5 5 5   9 5 5 4

Planes of Expression =   Physical (8), and Intuitive (5)

Mental	= 1
Physical	= 8
Emotional	= 1
Intuitive	= 5

Karmic lessons = 2–3–8; talents = 6

Number of 1's   = 1
Number of 2's   = 0 = missing digit
Number of 3's   = 0 = missing digit
Number of 4's   = 3
Number of 5's   = 6   (talents)
Number of 6's   = 1
Number of 7's   = 2
Number of 8's   = 0 = missing digit
Number of 9's   = 3

Age digit in 1971 = 54 + 55 = 9 + 10 = 10 = 1

Concords = Artistic (3–6–9)

Universal cycle = 9. Universal year (1971 = 9); Universal day = 5;
          Calendar day: January 4, 1971 = 5

Personal year = 8 (Aug. (8) + 27 (9) + 1971 (9) = 8

Personal day = 4 Personal day: Jan. (1) + 4 + 8 (personal year = 13 = 4

Name cycle = 16 letters = reduced 7

Key to character = 8

Predictions: 25, 26, 24, 25

Predictions: If you are figuring her chart on January 4, 1971, you must use
        the 1970 until her birthday on August 27, 1971.

OVERTONE	1st Period	2nd Period	3rd Period
	(Aug. 27.-Dec. 27)	(Dec. 27-May 27)	(May 27-Aug. 27)
1970	1970	1970	1970
17	54	25	8
1987 = 25	2024 = 26	1995 = 24	1978 = 25

Overtone = 25; First period = 26; Second period = 24; Third period = 25.

INTERPRETATION OF HER CHART

Notice the many nines in Martha Raye's original name of Margie Yvonne Reed. Having a soul's urge, personality and destiny number of nine indicates that her life evidently has been filled with many disappointments and losses. With her soul's urge of (11-7 = 9) she wants to be a perfectionist (7) appearing in the limelight (11) on the stage. Her aim is to entertain the public and serve her fellowman. Having the same personality number as her heart's desire indicates that she is exactly as she appears to be. Her destiny number of nine tells us that her purpose in life is to be impersonal.

This is not easy for an actress, for she is in a very competitive field. She must help others before thinking of herself (9). She must be a friend to all and give out love. She must make others laugh even though she may not always be happy inside.

Her present signature of eleven is made up of a soul's urge of eight and a personality of three. It still is harmonious with her birthpath, but the eleven master number puts her before the public in television, and it should be an inspiration to others. Her soul's urge of eight tells us that now she wants to make money, or handle big affairs. Her personality is that of a person well able to express herself (3). Again having a heart's desire as large and larger than her personality, she will wear well as a friend, for she is all she pretends to be. Remember, the original name still insists on being fulfilled no matter how many times she changes her name.

Her birthdate of August 27, 1916 totals seven. This is a difficult birthpath to handle. Again notice that her birthday is the 27th, which again can be reduced to nine. She must learn to develop the spiritual side of her nature. She should specialize. One field for her is acting. When a seven turns to acting she will excel at it. It is better for her not to seek or reach out for opportunity, but wait for it to be b.ought to her.

Being born on the 27th, she has a literary birthday. She is very psychic, but she must be careful for she could easily be disturbed. She should avoid excessive indulgences in any vices. Since she is a natural leader, she can't work in a subordinate position for others. She is very affectionate, but she is inclined to be somewhat nervous and erratic. An early marriage would be disappointing to her. She is in the artistic concord of 3-6-9, and would do well in any creative field of endeavor.

Martha Raye's power number is seven. She could specialize in some scientific field as an educator, writer, or as an inventor. She could also be a psychic, for her intuition should be well developed. She should have the advantage of being able to get the feel of an audience before she even begins to perform

Her pinnacle number for both the third and fourth period is seven. A seven pinnacle is again difficult to handle. Both sevens and nines augur much unhappiness for her unless she has learned to live for others. This is a good period for meditation. Money may be made under sevens and nines, but only after she has learned to accept material possessions for what they really are. The seven period may be hard on her health, as it demands much. She must develop poise and patience during the seven pinnacle. Losses may also be experienced.

She has a *0* challenge. This means she is an old soul who should be able to handle any problems. Either she will have no challenge to conquer, or everything will be a challenge for her. With so many sevens and nines, I would venture that her upward climb has been very difficult, filled with heartaches. She undoubtedly had to face many challenges. Not many individuals are forced to encounter and conquer so many sevens and nines.

Her planes of expression are the physical and intuitional. She is down-to-earth, practical, and can work hard, but she also is intuitive. She should at all times follow her hunches, for her ESP should be working for her.

Her karmic lessons are 2, 3, and 8. Most individuals have only one karmic lesson to overcome. There are three missing digits in her name, showing that in a past incarnation she was tactless and undiplomatic, which she must now overcome. The three shows that she formerly had difficulty expressing herself, and this would be especially a handicap for an actress. The eight shows that she had no sense of business values. Her talent, being six, shows that she can carry much responsibility. This is lucky, for she will need all the help she can get. Since she has accomplished so much, she evidently has learned her karmic lessons and is now free of obstacles, or at least many of them.

Her age digit is one, meaning the year 1971 would be a good time to start on a new venture, providing her other numbers indicate this also.

Her universal cycle is also a nine. This will operate during her

27th and 54th birthday. She is now in a transitional state, for she is passing into the digit of her year of eight. This will be in effect for the remainder of her life. Only through love and service can she overcome her many nines.

The universal year in 1971 in nine, and the day (January 4, 1971) is five. While her personal year is an eight (big business) and her personal day on January 4th is four (1 + 4 + 8 = 13 = 4), she should work hard.

Her original name at birth has sixteen letters, which reduces to seven. This means that her minor important years will be every seventh year, while her major year will be her sixteenth and any multiples of this number. Her next major cycle will be when she is sixty-four.

Her key to character of eight means that she will never know want, for she will always find a way out of her difficulties. This key often brings financial success in old age.

In figuring her predictions for the year, since the chart is set up on January 4, 1971, but her birthday will not be until August 27, 1971, you must use the previous year of 1970 for your calculations until her birthday.

The overtone for the year is twenty-five. This means a time of petty annoyances, difficulties, and sometimes an illness. It may put her in contact with elderly people, and may even end in an illness or death of an elderly person. With the first period of twenty-six, she must be careful of investments, for she could lose much. It again suggests a possible stroke of someone near her. It could be a splendid period financially, but usually with the 25 it points to trouble.

The second period of twenty-four shows that she will be in a love or home vibration during this period. With the twenty-five, it suggests a possible illness in the family.

The third and last period has another twenty-five vibration. This could indicate trouble and many hurdles to cross. Perhaps the following year will be more hopeful and successful for her. Luckily with her key to character of eight, she will find an answer to any difficulties she may encounter. They need not overwhelm her if she exercises her beautiful sixth sense of intuition.

SAMPLE NUMEROSCOPE OF BOB HOPE

(Interpretation of his chart)

Bob Hope's given name at birth is Leslie Townes Hope. He was born on May 29, 1903. You are figuring his chart on June 2, 1971.

$$\frac{1}{10}$$

$\overline{19}$	11	11	=	$\frac{(22 + 1)}{5}$ =	(Soul's Urge)

5 9 5	6 5	6 5

L E S L I E   T O W N E S   H O P E

3 1 3	2 5 5 1	8 7

7	13	15

7	4	6	**= 8**	(Personality)

8 +	6 +	8	**= 22**	(Destiny)

$\frac{6}{6}$	$\frac{11}{6 \quad 5}$		= (11 + 6) 8	(Soul's Urge)

B O B   H O P E

2 2 8 7	**= 10**	(Personality)

4 6		

10 + 8 = 18   9   (Present Signature)

Date of Birth:	May	29	1930	= (11 + 9)	11 (Birthpath)
	5	11	$\underline{13}$		
			4		

Birthday = 29th

Power No.: Destiny + Birthpath (22 + 11 = 6)

Challenge=   1

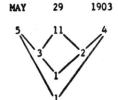

1st subchallenge   Second subchallenge

                                           Third and main challenge

                                           Fourth challenge

Pinnacle=   9

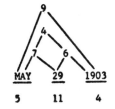

                                           Fourth pinnacle

                                           Third pinnacle

1st pinnacle   Second pinnacle

Figure 22-5

Pinnacles: 1   to   25   = 7
              26   to   35   = 6
              36   to   45   = 4
              46   on   = 9

L E S L I E   T O W N E S   H O P E

3 5 1 3 9 5   2 6 5 5 5 1   8 6 7 5

Planes of Expression: Physical (6) and Emotional (5)

Mental   = (1,8)   = 3
Physical   = (4,5)   = 6
Emotional   = (2,3,6) = 5
Intuitive   = (7,9)   = 2

Karmic Lessons =   4...talent   6

No. of 1's   = 2
No. of 2's   = 1
No. of 3's   = 2
No. of 4's   = 0

No. of 5's = 6
No. of 6's = 2
No. of 7's = 1
No. of 8's = 1
No. of 9's = 1

Age digit in 1971 = 9 (67 + 68 = 4 + 5 = 9)

Concord: 2, 4, 8, 11, 22

Universal cycle = 4 (year)

Universal year in 1971 = 9; Universal day = 8 (June 2, 1971)

Personal year = 7; Personal day = 6

Name cycle = 16 = 7

Key to character = 5

Predictions = 22, 32, 20, 23
If you are figuring your chart on June 2, 1971. Since the date is after his birthday, you should use the current year of 1971.

OVERTONE	First Period	Second Period	Third Period
	(May 29=Sept. 29)	(Sept. 29-Jan. 29)	(Jan. 29-May 29)
1971	1971	1971	1971
13	68	11	5
1984 = 22	2039= 32	1982 = 20	1976 = 23

Overtone = 22; First period = 32; Second period = 20; Third period = 23

INTERPRETATION OF BOB HOPE'S CHART

Bob Hope's destiny number of twenty-two is the highest master number possible. It means that he will have not only national but international contacts and success. He certainly has accomplished his purpose in life, for he has made many trips to foreign countries to entertain our armed forces. Also, he is well known in Europe and all over the world as a comedian and entertainer. His destiny number of twenty-two is made up of two eights and a six. The eights mean big business ventures, and the six applies to the community or country. He has invested in real estate deals (6) and many other big business projects (8). He is now worth millions of dollars due to his shrewd judgment (8).

His soul's urge number is 22-1 with an underlying 5. Again with the master number as part of his total, it means his secret desire is to be known widely as an individualist or unique person. He wants to do things in a creative way. The five shows that he is interested in everything new (5), change (5), and travel (5). He is restless and can't settle down. He's not as much a homebody or parent as he is a citizen of the world.

His personality number of eight suggests to others that he is systematic and orderly as well as being an excellent business man (8) and entertainer. He has an analytical mind (7), is practical (4), and loves to work for a cause (6).

His present signature consists of the 8-10-9 business trinity, which denotes success in business. If he had not been a comedian and prominent entertainer, he would have been equally successful in business as a financier. His new signature has a soul's urge of (11-6) with an underlying eight. His personality of ten shows him to be outstanding as a leader, and the new total of nine gives him a destiny of a philanthropist (9). He has contributed much in time and money to worthwhile organizations.

Bob Hope's birthday on May 29, 1903 again indicates with its (11-9 = 11) birthpath, that much is expected of him. He had to learn to be a performer on the platform (11) and be an inspiration (11) entertaining people (9) in a creative way. His birthday also is a master number (2 + 9 = 11). He has the talent to accomplish much. It is a very strong birthday showing that he can be prosperous, which he has proven. He is an extremist, either happy or depressed. With such strong master numbers, he had to learn to help others as well as straighten out his own path. Some people with this birthday become so engrossed in their own dreams that they ignore others. He may prefer many casual friends to a few intimate ones.

His power number is six, which is obtained by adding his destiny number (22) and his birthpath (11). It means that the latter part of his life will be taken up with service and humanitarian endeavors. He will be rewarded with love, protection, money, and accomplishment. He will still have responsibilities, for he will always have the duty to work for the good of others.

Since Bob Hope was sixty-eight on May 29, 1971 he is in the fourth or last pinnacle number of nine. While nine is often disappointing, it can be beneficial if he has learned true values. He should find this a satisfying pinnacle, since he has always helped his neighbor.

He has a one challenge, which means he had to learn to stand on his own feet and be a leader. He might have experienced opposition from his family in his youth. If he has conquered his challenge, which he evidently has, it will work for him giving him independence and creative ideas.

His planes of expression suggest he is physical (6) and emotional (5). His approach to a problem will be down-to-earth and practical, but he will let his feelings seep in and help govern his decision.

His karmic lesson is number four. In some previous lifetime he tried to escape doing hard work. Now it has been thrust upon him. Even in entertaining others he works very hard and untiringly. He has six fives, which serve as his talent giving him versatility, a youthful appearance, and a lively spirit. Since five is a physical number, and everyone has some fives, we deduct two from the total to get a true picture, but even four is a good amount.

His age digit in 1971 was nine, since he was both sixty-seven (4) and sixty-eight (5) in that year. A nine age digit means a time to discard the old, clean house, and make way for the new the following year. It is not an auspicious time to start anything new in a nine personal year, or an age digit of nine.

He is in the fire or business concord of 2, 4, 8, 11, and 22, since his birthday is on the twenty-ninth (11).

Bob Hope's universal cycle now and for the rest of his life will be the same as his year of birth, which reduces to four. It means he will always work hard, but to him it will be a happy and busy experience.

The universal year of 1971 vibrates to nine, which is a finishing year. The universal day (June 2, 1971) has a total digit of eight. This is a good day to transact business and organize affairs, be a good executive, and attend to duties.

His personal year in 1971 is seven, achieved by adding the month and day of his birth (May 29 to the year 1971) for a total of seven ($5 + 11 + 0 = 7$). His personal day is six. Add the current day (June (6) and the day (2) to his personal year of $(7) = (6 + 2 + 7 = 6)$. It would be an excellent year to study, or do some analytical research work. It is not inducive to entertaining or traveling. The personal day of six indicates it would be propitious to buy or sell property.

His total given name has sixteen letters, which again reduces to seven. Every seventh year should be of minor importance, while his sixteenth and any multiples of sixteen, should be a red letter year for him with some outstanding event.

Having a key to character of five, he is a restless person wanting constant change. This key offers much traveling. This he certainly has done. Sex may also be a strong influence.

PREDICTIONS

Bob Hope's overtone for the year of twenty-two indicates that he will be undecided what to do, for he could easily be misled. Twenty-two is a tricky vibration, and one in which his own judgment may not be good, for he will be too undecided about making any move. He should consult an expert before he makes any change or major decision. The first period of thirty-two, running from May 29, 1971 to September 29, 1971 states that his plans can easily be wrecked. The thirty-two could also refer to a nervous period filled with tension. It can be a favorable period depending on whether or not he makes the right move or decision. Looking at his chart, I would suggest that the decision could center around some illness, in which he should consult a specialist. The second period running from September 29th to January 29 is a good vibration, for it can bring success. While twenty is always a good vibration, when it is combined with the twenty-two it is problematical, and could turn in either direction for good or adverse conditions. The third period of 23, starting with January 29, 1972 and running to May 29, 1972 will be one in which a decision must be made. This again could refer to a health problem, as an illness may crop up and need a decision. This period may also involve some travel or legal affairs. It is a strange change. He may travel to distant countries or around the world under this vibration. It can mean protection and success, but it usually means the possibility of an illness.

I have demonstrated to you the relationship of numbers to your life. You can now apply the corresponding numbers to your name, finding through them many answers to your inner life. It is very imperative, however, in setting up your chart to understand that you must live your life to the fullest to achieve all of the things that you have come to do. Even though you have master numbers, they will be of no benefit to you unless you work to earn their possibilities or potencies.

This book was written to show you a way to help and understand yourself through numerology. May it give you the courage to see that life is exciting.